D1002293

Chekhov

J. B. PRIESTLEY

Anton
Chekhov

by J. B. Priestley

INTERNATIONAL
PROFILES

ISBN 0 249 44005 9

INTERNATIONAL PROFILES

General Editor: EDWARD STORER

English language editions published by:

International Textbook Company Limited
158 Buckingham Palace Road, London S.W.1

A. S. Barnes & Co. Inc., Cranbury, New Jersey 08512,
for sale in UNITED STATES OF AMERICA

International Textbook Company, 400 Pacific Highway, Crows Nest, NSW 2065
for sale in AUSTRALIA

Series Design: Melvyn Gill   *Pictorial Research:* F. G. Thomas
Colour Plates: Photoprint Plates Limited, Rayleigh, Essex
Covers: George Over Limited, London and Rugby
Paper: Frank Grunfeld (Sales) Limited, London
Text: Photoprint Plates Limited, Rayleigh, Essex
Binding: Butler and Tanner Limited, London and Frome

Author's Note

Anton Chekhov, 1883, from a portrait by his brother Nikolai *(Novosti)*

When this excellent series was being planned, I was asked to contribute to it, and I agreed to do so on one condition—that my subject should be Chekhov. There were various reasons for this choice. A dramatist myself, I had long enjoyed both admiration and affection for Chekhov's plays. Again, he had always seemed to me an unusually lovable writer. (It is a mistake to imagine that most writers are lovable human beings.) Finally, although I had read a good deal about him at one time or another and knew the main outlines of his life and career, I felt I needed to know more about him, and though this profile would have to be fairly brief, preparing to write it would give me the opportunity to become more closely acquainted with this truly remarkable man. And when I call him remarkable I am not thinking about him entirely in terms of his great talent as a storyteller, his original genius as a dramatist. There is more to Chekhov even than that. But clearly I cannot begin this profile by announcing one of its most important

I

conclusions. That must wait until the end. All I can say here is that I hope many readers will be tempted to explore further the breadth and depth of this fascinating character, as I have done with unflagging interest and pleasure. In a long writing life I have arrived at many decisions I have afterwards regretted, but my immediate choice of Chekhov, as a Profile subject, has certainly not been one of them.

A last point. In going through two lengthy biographies of Chekhov, and those of his letters that have appeared in an English translation, and various reminiscences of him by fellow Russian writers, I must have marked scores and scores of passages that I wanted to quote. But they would take up too much space. So for brevity's sake I have had to leave out almost all of them, short statements and pronouncements of my own taking their place. But these, unless I say so, are not based on guesswork: behind them are the direct quotations I have been compelled to omit. When I am hazarding a guess—and this is inevitable with a character as reserved and elusive as Chekhov was—I will avoid any pretence of complete certainty.

Chapter I

Anton Chekhov, 1884 (Novosti)

Anton Pavlovich Chekhov was born in 1860 at Taganrog, a small and decaying port on the Sea of Azov. His father was the son of a serf who had bought his freedom. His mother was the daughter of a cloth merchant. There were six children, five sons and a daughter —the younger sister, Masha, to whom Chekhov was closely attached throughout the whole of his life. He was the third son, and this gave him a kind of central position in the family that was important to him later on. His father kept, though too often neglected, a grocery store, which was open late, partly because it had one room that was a makeshift tavern for vodka drinkers. Chekhov's father was an unusual grocer if only because he had a passion for religious music and choir training, even turning his family into a miniature choir, singing services not only in church but also at home. There was a good deal of the peasant still in him; he could be harsh with his wife and sons, who at an early age had to spend long hours in the store. We know from what he wrote later that Chekhov resented this and disliked even more his father's almost brutally severe treatment of his mother, to whom Chekhov was always very close. From this side of his childhood he probably brought his suspicion of any harsh measures, any form of tyranny, his distaste for a sloppy and seedy provincial life (he had seen too much of it in the store), and a lasting contempt for the gloomy religious services he had had to learn by heart.

There was however another side to this early family life in Taganrog. It was not all store-keeping and hymn-singing. The boys played games, went for days in the country or out to sea, fishing, got up charades under the leadership of Anton, the liveliest and most ingenious of the lads, and listened for hours to their mother and an old nurse telling stories. Chekhov's boyhood was far from being unhappy, and if this seems to contradict what I have already written above, I cannot help it: Russian life has a bewildering trick of going into darkness and misery and then suddenly exploding into sunlight and gaiety. And nobody knew this better than Anton Chekhov.

However, the family business, like Taganrog itself, was not prospering. When Chekhov was fifteen, his two older brothers, Alexander and Nicolai, left for Moscow. Alexander, clever but unreliable and soon to become a hard drinker, contrived to earn a living of sorts as a journalist. Nicolai was an artist and not without talent, but he was lazy and unstable and permanently 'not understood'. Neither of them was to be of any help to his family, a fact that was to be of decisive importance in Anton Chekhov's life. The next year, 1876, his father faced bankruptcy, closed the store, and fled to Moscow to live with his sons there. Creditors claimed the house and all its furniture. Left almost penniless, Chekhov's mother soon followed her husband to Moscow, taking the three younger children with her. Anton—or 'Antosha' as he was called in the family—was to remain in Taganrog, lodging with the people who had taken over the Chekhov house. He had to stay behind, though he was only sixteen, to continue and then complete his course at the local high school. His family, now existing in appalling poverty in Moscow, could do nothing to help him. Indeed, he would have to sell the few remaining family possessions, odds and ends of pots and pans and the like, to help them. He would have to fend for himself, taking any little job out of school hours and doing some regular tutoring, and hoping that he might be invited to stay in the country—as he did on a Cossack farm—during the

4

longer school holidays. And not only did he keep himself, he was able to send occasional small sums to his mother, who complained bitterly of their distress in Moscow. Moreover, he soon began to create a new life for himself, making friends, meeting pretty girls, going to the theatre, exploring existence on the steppe, and starting to write after a fashion. In the summer of 1879 he was successful in his finals at the high school, which meant he could leave Taganrog for Moscow and enter the university there to read medicine. As we have seen so many photographs of Chekhov as a prematurely aged man, stooping, peering over his *pince-nez*, it is worth taking a glance at the statistics entered in his official travel permit at this time: *Age:* nineteen; *Height:* five feet eleven and three-quarter inches; *Hair and Eyebrows:* blond; *Eyes:* brown; *Nose, Mouth, Chin:* regular. He was in fact a tall, handsome, very lively and attractive youth.

5

These years, his later teens, when he was left behind in Taganrog, and had to look after himself, seem to me of immense importance in any study of Chekhov's life and character. (I believe anyhow that these later teens, almost always strongly formative, can be at least as significant as early childhood, and are too often ignored.) To begin with, they taught him to be independent, to stand up for himself, not to be parasitic. On the other hand, because he was left at sixteen to scrape together a few roubles for his distant family, he began to feel deeply responsible for his family, especially for his mother and sister; and this sense of responsibility never left him. He was the one they would have to depend upon. It is possible that his desire to study medicine was an extension of this feeling. After all, doctors are much-needed and highly responsible members of any society. So while young Anton Chekhov, far from being a prig, could enjoy convivial company, pretty faces, wine and music and play-acting, he could not surrender himself completely to such things, for he had to support himself and knew that soon he might have to support most of his family. Probably he knew already that curious mixture of easy sociability and aloofness, an inner detachment, which is to be found in his later life. Finally, because these later teens are so impressionable, and he came to know all manner of people in and around Taganrog, townsfolk from prosperous merchants to the riffraff of a port, Cossack landowners and peasants of the steppe, this wide acquaintance began to feed his memory and excite his imagination. So it is not surprising that Chekhov a little later, as a story-teller, showed himself to be so broadly-based: he already knew all kinds of people.

Chapter 2

Moscow c. 1880 (Mansell Collection)

When Anton Chekhov joined his family in Moscow, they were
living from hand to mouth in a four-room basement in a dingy
and rather disreputable quarter. His father now had a poorly
paid job in a warehouse at the other end of the city, only returning
to his family on Sunday. His harsh authority was crumbling away.
Anton brought three of his fellow students to be boarded and
lodged, which meant that the Chekhovs could begin to eat properly
again. As he showed from the first, he was ready to accept responsibility for the family and he was soon regarded as the head of it,
which he continued to be to the end of his life. He was no power-
monger but he had a strength of character lacking in his two elder
brothers, together with a natural generosity and sweet temper.
Nine persons shared that basement, but then most Russians have
a genius for coping with close quarters, domestic noise and bustle,
visitors who stay on and on. Even when, a little later, Anton was
able to earn money by writing, the student lodgers departed, and

the Chekhovs moved above ground in a better district, they kept open house, with everybody's friends, of different ages and types, for ever popping in and out. Anton was frequently in the middle of them, joking and playing tricks, yet he somehow contrived to keep up with his university work and to do more and more journalism for extra money. But then even in these early and high-spirited years, there was in Chekhov a steady determination, iron somewhere behind his easy smiling manner. From then onward he might appear to be entirely gentle, humorously self-deprecating, as indeed he nearly always was in company, but an unusual power of will was there. Without it he would never have succeeded, in later life, in writing exactly what he wanted to write. He might always appear to be giving in to more obviously masterful persons, but in fact he never did.

He worked hard and well at the university but he never really identified himself with it. Most of his new friends came from his life outside, from journalism and the arts. Apart from the actual work, he did not adopt the familiar role of the student. After Alexander II, a mild and reforming Czar, had been assassinated in 1881, there came with Alexander III the inevitable swing towards severe repression. This roused the more radical students. Meetings were held; committees formed; noisy demonstrations were organised. Chekhov may have attended some of the meetings, but he offered no oratory, joined no committee, took part in no public demonstration: he went on with his studies, his writing, his gregarious life at home. This is important because it helps us to understand his attitude of mind and behaviour later, when he was a celebrity. Chekhov was never a Czarist, a reactionary, nor even a conformist. He believed wholeheartedly in reform, and was at times himself an active reformer. But he was sceptical about large-scale political movements, distrusting abstractions and dogmatic ideologies. He was always quick to detect whatever was inflated and false in speech and behaviour, as his writing shows us. Nobly enthusiastic windbags were common enough in Russia, and Chekhov had no desire to leave his work to follow them. He did not want to be deceived by bogus personalities; he was not going to be bullied by party disciplines or collective authority; he wanted to preserve his independence and individual judgement. He was very different in outlook and temperament from William Blake, but I think that if he had known it he would have applauded Blake's famous dictum: *He who would do good to another must do it in Minute*

8

Particulars. General Good is the plea of the scoundrel, hypocrite, and flatterer. We have plenty of evidence that Chekhov never wearied of doing good in 'minute particulars'.

During his later terms as a medical student, Chekhov was very hard-pressed indeed. His hours were longer, he had to spend time in hospitals and clinics, yet he could not afford to neglect his humorous writing and journalism because he needed more and more money, not for himself but for his family. His younger brother Ivan no longer had to be supported because he was now a student teacher at a country school; but his sister Masha and young Mikhail had to finish their education, Nicolai too often spent more than he earned, and his eldest brother, Alexander, who had acquired a family of his own, was always in trouble. Chekhov's letters at this time ruefully describe his attempts to work, often far into the night, as a member of a noisy and demanding household. He was in fact recklessly driving himself too hard, busily shortening his life. Already divided between medicine and writing, he was still determined that he must qualify and transform himself into Dr A. P. Chekhov; and indeed as soon as he was entitled to do so, he put a sign on his door.

It is Anton Chekhov the storyteller and dramatist, not Dr A. P. Chekhov, who claims our interest. But the two cannot be entirely separated, for various reasons I shall mention later. What I will do here and now is to consider briefly the medical side of Chekhov's life. He never seriously settled down to practise as a doctor because he soon preferred to earn his living by writing. Even so, he thought of himself as a literary man who was also a doctor. Until his very last years, the physician in him was never banished. And indeed, as we shall see later, when he owned a country estate and was surrounded by peasants in urgent need of medical attention, he often worked as hard and long as most country doctors did, frequently under worse conditions, entirely out of charity. Would he ever have succeeded professionally as Dr A. P. Chekhov? Not as a surgeon, for he would never have achieved the iron nerve and manual dexterity that surgery demands, but his early experiences suggest he might have been an excellent physician, because he soon showed promise in diagnosis and had a sympathetic understanding of his patients. (But a physician who was himself the victim of tuberculosis would hardly be fashionable.) However, the influence of his years of training as a medical student remained with him, together with his acceptance of himself as a doctor, and

Anton Chekhov the writer would not have been the same without them.

It is the writer we must now consider. Chekhov's beginnings were very humble indeed. They could hardly have been anything else. He was a young medical student from a distant province, outside any literary circle in Moscow, unacquainted with any established men of letters. At first he was not even *trying* to be a writer. He merely wanted to earn some quick money to keep his family going. Literary work that took time and trouble was quite impossible. He could only do little pieces that could be dashed off in a corner. Fortunately there was a market for such things. Cheap magazines, with titles like *Dragonfly, Alarm Clock, Fragments,* were numerous and popular at that time, and though they paid very badly—and sometimes suddenly ceased to pay at all—they were always looking for new contributors. (One or two of them regularly printed brief criticisms of pieces submitted to them.) Chekhov sent them tiny tales, comic sketches and parodies, articles on miscellaneous subjects, and gradually as he came to be known, even though he used various pseudonyms (*Antosha Chekhonte* was his favourite), he was allowed to do a fair amount of regular journalism, including some reviewing and dramatic criticism. He soon came to know a number of his fellow journalists, mostly older men who drank hard but were not without a feeling for literature. Moreover, his search for material for short tales and articles took him everywhere in Moscow and enabled him to study an enormous variety of men and women. In other circumstances he might have been already engaged on some portentous literary task, working in a quiet library, but in my opinion these two or three years of hack writing, done under high pressure, were really a far better apprenticeship. Young Chekhov learnt fast, was sharply critical of himself as well as of others, and would soon be able to make the best use of this wealth of experience.

There is a point here worth making. During his last two years at the university, Chekhov was writing hard, chiefly to please a friendly editor called Leikin, but he was still thinking about qualifying in medicine and not about a literary career. A young man his age solemnly entering literature would probably be attempting to write like Tolstoy or Dostoievsky or following some fashion praised in the critical journals. Chekhov was outside all this. By trying to earn some money, without a thought of literary fashion and fame, by trying to please editors who immediately

Anton Chekhov with his brother Nikolai, 1880 *(Novosti)*

rejected anything long-winded and high-faluting, Chekhov began to create his own original literature. He approached his work from a different direction. Then he gradually asserted his own natural good taste and fresh feeling, together with his sense, sharpened by his scientific study, of what was true and what was false in life. So during these years in the early 1880s, there are already glimpses of the Chekhov we know, immature though he might be. He started to feel his way beyond humorous little tales towards stories that were brief enough but explored greater depths, that seemed coolly objective and yet released much feeling, that created an atmosphere in a few short sentences. His occasional dramatic criticism increasingly encouraged him to rebel against what was accepted in the Moscow theatres, writing and acting that seemed to him quite false. He felt there ought to be another and better way to write for the Theatre, and he kept this in mind even while dashing off some unambitious but effective little 'vaudeville' pieces.

Life was not easy in Russia, with its censorship and suspicious bureaucracy and permits, but it had its compensations. It had a certain social flexibility and generosity that I doubt if a poor young man like Chekhov would have found in London or Paris in the early 1880s. In spite of his youth, Ivan Chekhov was appointed master of his school at Voskresensk, a small country town not too far from Moscow, and he was given a whole house to himself. So there the family went to spend the summer, and as soon as Anton had passed his finals he went there too. Food was cheap and plentiful out in the country; entertaining agreeable neighbours was easier than in Moscow; and the sociable Chekhovs soon made any number of new friends, including some of the military stationed in the district (*The Three Sisters?*). Then a young doctor from Zvenigorod, another small town in the neighbourhood, invited the newly qualified Dr Chekhov, in the casual Russian manner, to fill in for him during his holiday. This meant some useful work, more new experiences, more new friends. Among them was a landowner called Kiselev or Kiselyov, whose wife, the daughter of the director of the Moscow Imperial Theatre, was a writer herself. The Kiselevs had many writers, musicians, painters, among their friends, were immensely hospitable, and Chekhov spent more than one summer with them, often passing his days roaming round the estate, meeting the various odd types employed there and offering his services to the sick.

I have already pointed out that Chekhov's journalism in Moscow, his search everywhere for promising topics, enabled him to meet all manner of people. But the time he spent in those two small towns, Vroskesensk and Zvenigorod, his rambling days and talkative nights at the Kiselevs, were of even greater value to him as a writer. It was here above all that he first encountered the persons and situations, the styles of life, that we find, not of course directly copied but filtered through the mind of a creative artist, in so many of his tales and in his strongest plays. After all, Moscow and Petersburg rarely appear in his more mature stories, and as for his plays, *The Seagull, Uncle Vanya, The Three Sisters,* and *The Cherry Orchard* do not take us into any city nor anywhere near one. We might say that while it was young Dr A. P. Chekhov who first went to spend the summer in the country, the man who came back from it to Moscow was Anton Chekhov, writer.

Name-plate: Doctor A. P. Chekhov (SRC Photo Library)

Chapter 3

Chekhov's house in Moscow *(Novosti)*

When I said above that it was Dr Chekhov who went into the country and Anton Chekhov the writer who came back, I was describing attitudes of mind, inner states, and not dealing with the facts of his life. Actually, in 1885 and for some time afterwards, Chekhov conducted a practice of sorts in Moscow, still living with his family but soon in better quarters—at last he had a study of his own. Few young doctors at that time could find a lucrative practice and Chekhov was probably worse off than most of them. There were two good reasons for this. He had too many of his spendthrift bohemian acquaintances among his patients. And though not a fool about money as his brothers Alexander and Nicolai were, he was altogether too sympathetic and generous to be successful as a fee-claimer. In fact, at this time, with Masha and Mikhail still being educated, Masha as a teacher, Mikhail as a law student, and the family still more or less keeping open house, the Chekhovs were often hard pressed for money. Anton was devoting as much time and energy to writing as before, though much harassed by his tuberculosis, which was better in the country and always worse in Moscow. But now he was tired of running around and then dashing off little funny pieces. He wanted to do longer and more serious stories, even though these were always in danger of being censored and so becoming a dead loss financially. The writer was at last taking over from the hack journalist.

It was during these years, 1885–90, that Chekhov's fortunes and reputation changed most dramatically. In 1885 he was an impecunious young doctor hardly known as a writer. In 1890, when he made a complete break by travelling across Siberia to visit the island of Sakhalin, he was not only widely popular but already a literary celebrity. (And so, of course, praised, flattered, sought-after, and also savagely attacked by the envious.) If there was one supreme turning-point in Chekhov's career, it came quite early in this period, in 1886, when he was invited to pay his first visit to Petersburg. It was of course—as it still is—an exciting place, one of the most beautiful cities in the world. It was also then not only the political and social capital of Russia but also the centre of its cultural life. Its best publishers, editors, newspapers and magazines were to be found there. The kind of stories Chekhov wanted to write, very different from the light stuff demanded by Moscow's humorous little magazines, had a fair chance of being appreciated and accepted in Petersburg. And so it turned out, for it was there that Chekhov met Suvorin, who was to be his editor and publisher, financial backer and close friend for many years.

Alexy Sergeyevich Suvorin (1834–1912) was a self-made man who had written stories and plays but whose real and quite re-markable success was as a kind of *entrepreneur*, a businessman-cum-showman, of literature and journalism, a go-getting type familiar enough in the West but unusual in nineteenth-century Russia. His newspaper, *New Times*, well written but tending to be reactionary in its opinions, had the largest circulation in the country. He also owned a publishing house, a magazine and a number of bookshops, and he enjoyed a monopoly of bookselling for the railways. A bulky, expansive and masterful man, he was wealthy and enjoyed spending his money on luxurious living both at home in Petersburg and on his frequent visits abroad. He took up Chekhov with enthusiasm—it was not long before they were close friends—and paid him handsomely both as editor and publisher. But this was not unmixed good fortune for Chekhov.

Many progressives, especially among the younger writers, resented Suvorin and his reactionary *New Times*, and began to regard Chekhov, uncommitted politically, with some suspicion.

On the other hand, shortly after his first stay in Petersburg, Chekhov had received a long letter, the first of its kind he had ever received, from Grigorovich, a solidly established novelist of peasant life and now in his sixties. He warmly praised Chekhov's originality and the remarkable accuracy and truth of his descriptions of people and nature, but warned him against writing too much, under various pseudonyms, and often too hurriedly, urging him to take greater care of his fine talent. This letter, both in its praise and its blame, made an immediate profound impression on Chekhov, who after all was only twenty-six. He was immensely grateful for the recognition of his talent and did not shrink from the older man's reproaches. 'If I have a gift which must be respected,' Chekhov declares in his reply, 'then before the purity of your heart I confess that I have not respected it up to now. I felt that I had such a gift, but I had grown accustomed to regarding it as insignificant.' His family and most of his Moscow friends, he goes on to say in effect, had never taken his writing seriously; they thought of him as a physician; and, he adds ruefully, 'No one has lost more sleep than I have over the fable of hunting two hares at one time.'

He had still to hunt the two hares, even while passing the summer in the country near the Kiselevs, for the peasants came for their usual free treatment. His first real collection of stories, *Motley Tales,* and the first of many that appeared regularly afterwards, was published this summer of 1886, and was pleasantly noticed, except by one influential critic, Skabichevsky, who made a savage personal attack on Chekhov. A long time afterwards, talking to Maxim Gorky, Chekhov said: 'For twenty-five years I've read criticisms of my stories, and I don't recall a single remark of any value nor have I heard a single piece of good advice. Once, however, Skabichevsky produced an impression on me—he wrote that I would die in a ditch, drunk.' It is a curious thing about authors— and I write out of fifty years' experience—that whereas they soon forget the praise they remember the unpleasantest notices of their work.

There is something ironical, indeed quite Chekhovian, in the contrast between the impression he made upon others, many of them young writers meeting him for the first time, and what he

Верзила. Фельдшерица N. изъ Петерб. рожд. курсовъ, идейная, влюбилась въ учителя X., думалъ, что онъ тоже идейный, труженикъ во вкусъ повѣстей и рома новъ, которыя она такъ любила. *Онъ мало по малу ока- добродушнымъ и недалекимъ* зался пьяницей, явился; ——————— *его соли* ли, онъ сталъ рѣзъ при женъ, обнядъ ее. Это былъ наростъ, вродѣ саркомы, которыи исощалъ ее совершенно. Какъ то она встрѣтила инж. помѣщи- ковъ, ѣздила къ нимъ каждый день; было неловко плясать ей — и они подарили ея мужу костюмъ, къ ея великой досадѣ. Живя съ мужемъ, она сда- *Онъ подолгу пилъ чай и это ее возмущало.* ла зощенкой, некрасивой, злой; топала ногами и кричала ему: — "Оставь меня, низкій человѣкъ!" Ненавидѣла его. Она работала, а ему платили *что кого пилъ она, кого женить, не брала.*

Молодой человѣкъ собралъ милліонъ марокъ, легъ на нихъ и застрѣлился.

лампадка, вспыхивают волосы

"Эти женщины...". Я женился 20 лѣтъ, не выпилъ во всю мою жизнь ни одной рюмки водки, не вы- курилъ ни одной папиросы". Послѣ того, какъ онъ соврѣшилъ, его полюбили и сдали ему больше

was actually feeling and suffering in private. He was so handsome, so charming, so amusing and original, so captivating to women, they all declared. Yet at this time, out of sight he was coughing and spitting blood, and he was plagued, as he was to be for many years, by painful haemorrhoids. He worried about his two older brothers: Alexander, now in Petersburg again and with another child, was writing nonsense and piling up debts; Nicolai, soon to die, was now a wreck. Then, in spite of Suvorin and *New Times*, money was going out faster than it was coming in. Finally, the letter from Grigorovich, even though the amiable old fellow became a family friend, burned in Chekhov's memory. He had a fine original talent—and this was beginning to be widely acknowledged—but he was not treating it with the respect he deserved. He was behaving to it not like a lover but a whore-master. Inner confusion, doubt, feelings of guilt, tempted him to overplay in public the role of the newly discovered young genius, as some of his friends and colleagues noticed at this time; but alone with himself he felt increasingly dissatisfied, sadly at a loss.

Though always eager for change and travel, Chekhov in 1887 probably decided to revisit Taganrog and then the Don Steppe to escape from this heavy mood, to find material and inspiration for new and better stories. In Taganrog, where he was welcomed as a celebrity, he stayed with his old Uncle Mitrofan, of whom he was very fond. But he had to sleep on a couch too small for him, the food upset him and he had to keep running out into the night, having no alternative indoors, to relieve himself. Though occasionally moved by childhood memories, he found Taganrog even more run-down and slatternly than he expected it to be, a place neglected by too many stupid and lazy people. He was glad to leave it to stay with old Cossack friends of his youth, and to travel day after day across the huge Steppe, passing two nights at the Holy Mountains Monastery, where 15,000 pilgrims arrived to celebrate a feast day. One young Cossack farmer, after reading a few brief treatises, decided in favour of the new scientific farming, which resulted in wholesale slaughter. Chekhov wrote: 'They kill sparrows, swallows, hornets, ants, magpies and crows to prevent them from eating the bees; then they kill the bees to keep them from spoiling the blossoms of the fruit trees; finally they cut down the fruit trees so they will not exhaust the soil.' Various odd characters and situations suggested stories that he wrote afterwards. In one of them he transferred his feeling for the magnitude and mystery of the Steppe to a young boy, travelling across it for the first time; and his unusually long *The Steppe: the Story of a Journey*, begun in 1887, is one of his earliest masterpieces.

However, the heavy mood returned after his visit to the South, and though he might be gay enough in company his letters to close friends like Madame Kiseleva suggest a darkening pessimism. Even the rapturous reception of *The Steppe*, which brought him new and warmer praise from his fellow writers, did not leave him at peace with himself. Restless and dissatisfied, he began to consider writing a novel. Suvorin had now guaranteed him a monthly income; his work for *New Times* gave him an excuse for fairly frequent visits to Petersburg, where Suvorin began to make much of him and saw to it that other writers did too. But the mood persisted, even surviving two enjoyable holiday journeys, one to the Ukraine, the other to the Crimea. Even so, he could be freed from gloom temporarily by the new challenge, the urgency and limelight glare of the Theatre. He was asked to write a real full-length play instead of another humorous one-acter, for a Moscow company, and he 'went to bed, thought of a theme', as he himself declared, and then wrote the play in the next ten days.

This was *Ivanov*, rather oddly described as 'a comedy in four acts'. Chekhov for once responded eagerly to all the fuss, the praise of actors, the paragraphs in the press, the management's talk of big money. But the rehearsals alarmed him by their inadequacy, though he did his best to help the actors. (Chekhov had a natural sense of the Theatre.) The Moscow first night took place in November 1887, and it seemed to him to be artistically a disaster. The play was dreadfully under-rehearsed; many of the actors did not know their lines and wildly ad-libbed; and several were drunk. Nevertheless, there was enthusiasm as well as sheer noise in the audience, sharply divided in its opinion. The notices reflected this division—and were 'mixed'. However, at this time, any ambitious dramatist looked to Petersburg, which had far better directors, players and critics than Moscow. Chekhov went there himself, taking copies of the play with him. Now a celebrity, he was fêted, made new friends among well-known writers, and there was endless excited talk about *Ivanov* and its production in Petersburg. Nevertheless, it was not until the end of January 1889 that the play opened there, at the important Alexandrinsky Theatre. It was Chekhov himself who was responsible for the long delay. He wanted to revise the play thoroughly but turned aside to do other things, including some very successful one-acters, and he was still revising it when he went to Petersburg for the production. This time it had been properly rehearsed and was well-acted, and the result was a triumph, far beyond Chekhov's expectations. Secretly he had come to dislike *Ivanov*: he knew now that this was not what he wanted in the Theatre, though he was not ready yet to fulfil his deepest demands. 'The truly powerful talent' and the 'great dramatic talent' they were so busy acclaiming in Petersburg (and he rushed away from it the day after the first night) was not the talent that Anton Chekhov knew now he would have to nurse.

The trouble with *Ivanov* is not that it was written too quickly— after all, it was extensively revised—but that it was *created* too quickly, overnight as we have seen. Its people were never brooded over. Its scenes did not gradually emerge in the dramatist's mind but were hastily concocted, with an eye to obvious theatrical effect. It has almost the same relation to the real Chekhov as the cover of its paperback has to many a serious novel. Too much of it is crude and overdone, especially in the two middle acts. The very end, Ivanov's suicide, is so hurriedly forced that we feel resentment instead of compassion. The melodramatic soliloquies are out of key and tone. Ivanov, as a specimen of the empty spiritless Russian intellectuals of the 8os, is a good *idea* but he is merely put together, not really created. And Lyov, the 'honest' young doctor, is a type, not a living character. Even so, there are moments when the young girl in love, Sasha, her father, the amiable drunk Lebedyev, and that absurd pair, Count Shabelsky and Borkin the steward, bring us closer to the Chekhov of *The Three Sisters* and *The Cherry Orchard*. But in the 1880s Chekhov was not quite ready for the Theatre, and it is even more certain that the Theatre was not ready for him. All Petersburg might be applauding *Ivanov*, but he hurried away and then refused to talk about the play because the dramatist in him was already beginning to grow, to dream of his maturity.

One of his most fervent admirers in Petersburg was Lidiya Avilova, handsome and vivacious and only twenty-four, though already the wife of a civil servant and the mother of a son. She was trying to write herself; she asked Chekhov to advise her; and she also immediately fell in love with him. ('Something exploded in my soul,' she declared, years later.) In memoirs written in her old age—they were published in 1949—she acclaimed that she and Chekhov enjoyed a long love affair, which had to be kept secret. But such evidence as we have suggests that while she may not have been deliberately inventing a passionate relationship, in remembering her own feelings she began to imagine a romantic attachment on his part that probably never existed. So far I have said nothing about Chekhov's relations with women. Like most imaginative young men, he was highly susceptible, enjoyed the company of pretty girls and attractive lively women, and had, mostly in Moscow, a number of light-minded, rather casual affairs. During his later twenties, his mother was always urging him to marry; he spoke of marriage himself; and at one time there was talk of his being engaged to the daughter of a merchant. But he did not want a rich wife and could not afford a poor one. He still had some of his family to support; between literature and medicine he was driven hard; and there was his tuberculosis to fight. Had he been the victim of a grand passion, if there had been some woman he could not bear to be parted from, his history would have been different. But while susceptible and eagerly appreciative of feminine charm, there was in Chekhov a certain detachment, belonging to both the doctor and the writer in him, that prevented him from falling headlong in love. Though in his work, especially as it developed, he could bring understanding and compassion to his account of women, in his ordinary talk he was apt to speak lightly and rather cynically about them. This was partly a reaction, which can also be found in his work, against bogus Russian sexual romanticism, deathless loves that might be over in six months. He tended to overplay honest scepticism. A little later (but before he met Olga Knipper), with one or two delightful girls, to whom he was really as devoted as they were to him, he carefully adopted a teasing avuncular manner, which at times they must have secretly detested. He makes us feel that behind the compliments, fun and kisses he was on his guard. He was protecting against intrusion and any weakening a central private area of responsibility for his family and his health, for his duty as a medical man, and above all for the creative writer in him who demanded more and more serious attention. Woman had to wait until work was done.

Professor Simmon's full-scale biography of Chekhov is so rich in detail, sympathy, insight, is so sure a guide, that I am astonished to find anything in it I cannot accept. But when he writes 'the years 1885 to 1889 were among the happiest in Chekhov's relatively short life', he seems to me to be defying much of the evidence he has himself carefully assembled. True, Chekhov was no longer a poor man, living in great discomfort; his talent was widely recognized and praised he had made many new friends, some of them the best-known creative artists in the country—Tchaikovsky, for example. But he was not long happy with himself. His more intimate letters are often despairing. He can declare himself like the blackest of the pessimists or another desperate Ivanov. As soon as he considered himself primarily a writer, a serious literary artist with a growing reputation, he had to face the problem of what we should now call 'commitment'. Whose side was he on? (It was assumed that he must take a side, write with a purpose, adopt some general ideas or ideals.) Certainly he was no reactionary like his friend Suvorin and most of the contributors to *New Times*. In practical matters he was more aware of what was at fault, more keenly progressive and eager for reform, than his fellows who were political and social rebels, deeply 'committed', and beginning to be suspicious of him. (He was equally suspicious of them, chiefly because he felt they were too abstract, too automatically dogmatic, too politically-minded to see life freshly and sharply.) But he was worried by the charge that he had no standpoint of his own, no general idea—and it was brought particularly against his ambitious *A Dreary Story* of 1889. Also, he knew that several stories written a little earlier had shown a Tolstoyan influence that was in fact false to his own deepest feelings and growing convictions.

There was every excuse for this influence. Tolstoy was the only literary giant left on the scene, and Chekhov who had yet to meet him admired him enormously. Tolstoy had now been converted to his vastly over-simplified view of life and art, and was bringing out *The Death of Ivan Ilyich*, his play *The Power of Darkness*, and then *The Kreutzer Sonata*. The old magic still worked for Chekhov, though he was irritated by so many of Tolstoy's dogmatic but quite unscientific pronouncements. It is worth pointing out here that one reason for the rapid growth of Chekhov's reputation, once his work was known in literary circles, was that by these later 1880s both Dostoievsky and Turgenev had quitted the scene, younger men of talent like Gorki or Bunin had not yet arrived, there was a lack of major figures to admire or denounce—and here was young Anton Chekhov, so gifted, so fresh and original. Chekhov was to have the worst luck in his life, racked by consumption for years, dying so early; but I take nothing away from his genius if I add that in his career as a writer he was unusually fortunate. The little tales he wrote to earn money soon brought him great popularity. When he began to write seriously, he arrived on the literary

Anton Chekhov, 1888 (*Novosti*)

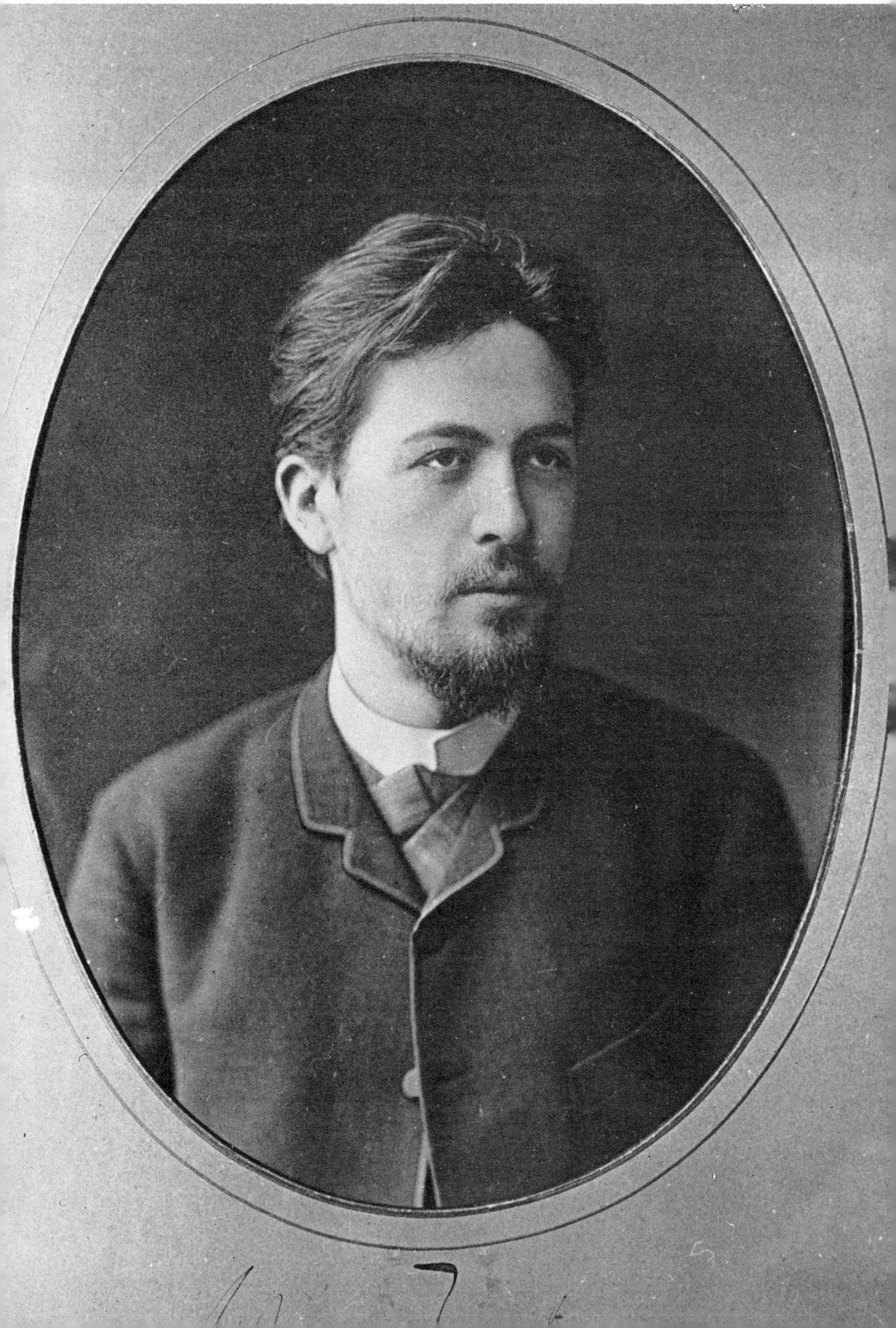

scene at just the right time, when there was plenty of room for the growth of a new reputation. And when later, as a dramatist, he needed a different kind of Theatre to do his work justice, the Moscow Art Theatre was created—just in time. He was an unlucky man but a lucky writer.

The old ease and fecundity, enabling him to dash off story after story in any circumstances, had vanished by 1889. It was a sterile and deeply unsatisfactory year. After months of suffering from the final stages of tuberculosis, his brother Nicolai died. Anton was not even there when he did die, because after attending him for weeks and weeks on end Anton had gone away for a much-needed break to stay with friends. Poor Nicolai had been at his best during the student days, when he did brilliant little sketches to illustrate Anton's funny little tales and articles. After that he had drifted from being a nuisance, with all his drinking and laziness, into the last tragic phase. Through it all, though often being sharply critical, Chekhov had been deeply attached to him: this was the first death in the family, and Chekhov had not even been there at the end and could not help feeling guilty. Once more, he played rather apathetically with the idea of writing a novel. He turned to the stage again and was able to add to his successful repertoire of one-acters or 'vaudevilles'; but he was chiefly at work, rather sporadically, on the play he had originally suggested as a collaboration with Suvorin. The latter soon dropped out, and left to himself Chekhov abandoned the idea of writing a more or less conventional comedy in four acts. He began to cut down the number of characters (he had used far too many in *Ivanov*), to go deeper into his people, to make them explain themselves in a new way, and to banish obvious theatricality. In this play, which he called *The Wood Demon*, he was in fact moving, if rather uncertainly, towards the later dramatic form that he made entirely his own. Indeed, most of us have been held and fascinated by what *The Wood Demon* became after much later revision—namely, *Uncle Vanya*.

In spite of some touches of melodrama that Chekhov had not removed from *The Wood Demon*, probably as a sop to convention, it was rejected in Petersburg, leaving Chekhov hurt and angry, and when it was produced by a new company in Moscow towards the end of 1889, it failed badly. Worried about 'commitment', accusing himself of having fallen too easily to Tolstoy's influence, finding his attempt to bring something new into the Theatre

24

derided or denounced, without any desire to write the stories everybody told him he ought to write, Chekhov was now suffering from what Americans like to call 'writers' block'. 1890 brought him the feeling that what he needed was a complete break. It was then that he astonished his public and bewildered his family and friends by announcing that he would visit the penal colonies of Sakhalin, far away off the Pacific coast, with all Siberia between them and Moscow. This immense and reputedly dangerous journey—at that time there was still no Trans-Siberian railway—was to be part of a scientific and humanitarian enterprise, not at all a literary affair. Chekhov made it plain from the first that he was going as a doctor, to compile statistics and make a medical report, and not as a storyteller and dramatist in search of new impressions and material. Waving away all objections, Dr A. P. Chekhov, before setting out, gave himself an arduous programme of reading and research. He fixed his mind on Sakhalin and its convicts, as if literature and the drama hardly existed.

Probably few men, certainly very few writers, have had a smaller capacity for self-deception than Anton Chekhov. He could coolly observe himself as he could others. But this surprising decision, not only to visit Sakhalin but to compile a researcher's report on its penal settlements, was not without some element of self-deception. True, it was a deeply humane project; he would have to sacrifice precious money and even more precious time. Even if there were no brigands to be faced, as his friends imagined, there would certainly be much discomfort, probably downright hardship, on the long journey across Siberia, undoubtedly an ordeal for a man in his precarious state of health. So in one sense it was a gallant decision. Yet it could reasonably be branded as an escape, a hasty flight from the unsolved problems of his literary career. A 'committed' Dr A. P. Chekhov, preparing to examine the penal settlements, could take over from the 'uncommitted', bewildered, uncertain Anton Chekhov, writer. He was still capable of doing some cool medical and social research, as his stay at Sakhalin showed (even though he found it a hell on earth), but that he was now acting out of his essential character is proved by the fact that on his return he could not help delaying his report. Indeed, it was not finished until 1893, when it was quietly published and then largely forgotten, even by Chekhov himself.

However, he arranged to do some newspaper articles on Sakhalin. He set out in April 1890, with no official credentials, depending

25

Map of Sakhalin island used by Chekhov (SRC Photo Library)

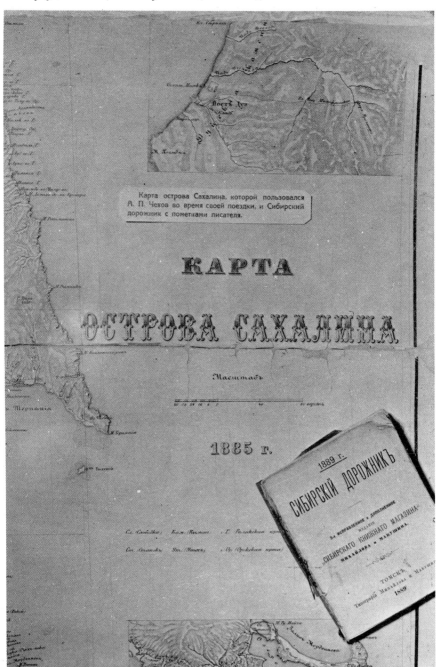

simply on his status as a journalist; and he finally reached Sakhalin towards the middle of July. His letters describing the journey across Siberia make lively reading. When he could not take a lake or river steamer, he had to hire or buy horses and various vehicles to move along the appalling roads, often with food and accommodation equally appalling. But the final stage of the journey, a considerable part of it, was by steamer down the Amur river, delightful after the Siberian rough and tumble. He spent three busy months on Sakhalin, travelling all over the island, gathering statistics (officially he was attempting a census and this gave him an excuse to move around and talk to people) and making the acquaintance of thousands of chained prisoners and penal colonists. (Many of their grateful letters to him, after he returned to Russia, exist in a Moscow Lenin Library collection.) If the plight of the men was horrifying, that of their women, often living by prostitution, and of their neglected children was even worse. It is likely that Chekhov's articles, rather than his long-delayed book, did something to initiate much-needed reforms; and it is certain that on his return Chekhov himself did everything he could to help the wretched prisoners and their families. Probably his most successful enterprise, in which he was joined by his brother Ivan the schoolmaster, was the collection and dispatch of suitable books for the education of the Sakhalin children.

Heartsick and homesick, he left the horrible island in October, before the grim winter set in, taking a passage in a steamer bound for Odessa. He visited Hong Kong, Singapore and Ceylon, which he loved, endured the heat and tedium of the Red Sea and the Suez Canal, enjoyed his glimpse of Constantinople, landed thankfully at Odessa and climbed into the train for Moscow. Home again—at last!

Chapter 4

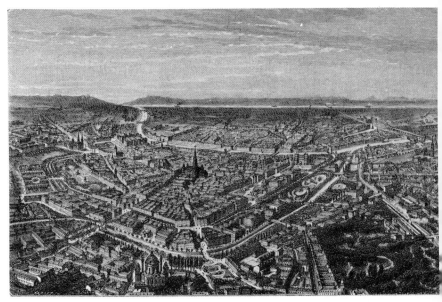

Vienna in 1871 (Mansell Collection)

Like many another homecoming, Chekhov's soon proved to be
disappointing. Inevitably there was a lot of fuss, first in Moscow
and then in Petersburg, with admiring visitors arriving by the
score and ambitious hostesses inviting him to be their guest of
honour. No doubt he was—in our old-fashioned term—'the lion
of the season', but Chekhov never enjoyed being lionized. Moreover,
he began to notice that behind the admiring attention and all the
compliments there was a great deal of envy and sour criticism,
especially among journalists and youngish fellow writers. He wrote
his sister Masha from Petersburg: 'I'm surrounded by a thick
atmosphere of ill-feeling.' Some of this was due to jealousy of his
friendship with the rich and influential Suvorin. It was however a
genuine friendship, which Chekhov took care never to exploit in
their publisher-author relationship. (In fact he was now so popular
with readers that he was offered, and refused, better terms than
those he had agreed with Suvorin.) It was obvious to the older man

28

that Chekhov, then his guest, was feeling rather unhappy and restless, disinclined to settle down to work, so Suvorin proposed that they should go on a tour of Western Europe. Chekhov refused at first—he had been away for eight months and needed to earn money, not spend more and more of it—but after some unsatisfactory weeks away from Petersburg, suddenly and delightedly, knowing that Suvorin and *New Times* would advance the money, he agreed to go. In mid-March 1891, they set out, in grand Suvorin-style, for Vienna.

The cleanliness, elegance, apparent freedom of Vienna enchanted Chekhov. Venice followed and only heightened his rapture. It would be easy for a poor and oppressed Russian, he wrote to his brother Ivan, to go out of his mind in this world of beauty, wealth and freedom. But his ecstatic mood vanished during their tour of other Italian cities. The weather was bad; the food was too rich; he was beginning to feel exhausted; and keeping up with the Suvorin-style was costing him far too much. However, they went on to Nice and Monte Carlo, where Chekhov, in the true Russian manner, gambled away money he could not afford to lose (and was rather pleased at himself), and arrived in Paris on May Day. He liked Paris but would have enjoyed it more if he had not felt it was time he went home and did some work. It is significant that Chekhov, who was not a puritan and who delighted in the unfamiliar luxury of life in Vienna, soon began to react against the wealthy, hot-house atmosphere of the French Riviera— an atmosphere, he wrote to his sister, 'that offends your sense of decency and vulgarizes nature, the moon, and the sound of the sea'. Nothing could corrupt Anton Chekhov.

That summer the family crammed themselves into a tiny *dacha* in the country, but then, to Anton's relief, found they could rent a whole upper floor in Bogimovo, an old and gigantic mansion, with a beautiful garden and an enormous park. Here they could entertain old and new friends, and among the latter—an admirer of Chekhov's stories—was a zoologist called Wagner, busy with some research work on spiders. I mention him because he and Chekhov spent many an evening eagerly discussing scientific subjects, and much of Wagner's character, mind, outlook, found their way into Chekhov's fiction of that period. In spite of the holiday atmosphere, he was now working hard, only too well aware of the debts hanging over him. He got up early, gave himself some coffee, then worked continuously until the middle of the morning. Usually he began writing again in the late afternoon, until it was time for supper. He kept returning to his book about Sakhalin but made little headway with it, for now it seemed a dreary task standing between him and his creative work. He was writing *The Duel*, almost as long as a novel, but would break away from it to produce some short tales. Much of his fiction at this time presents a sharp contrast, in various situations, between the scientist, cool, precise, objective, perhaps public-spirited, and the loose-living, shallow artist, the lazy and empty intellectual, the self-centred pessimists and 'Moscow Hamlets'. Lacking his usual objectivity and breadth of sympathy, most of it is below the level of his best work. For example, *The Grasshopper* describes how a foolish young wife is enticed away by a 'romantic' and 'glamorous' painter, really a selfish sensualist. She despises her patient loving husband, a medical scientist, who is actually a great man. This story, based on real persons and events, created a lively scandal in Moscow and did Chekhov much harm. And though the story has its moments, it has always seemed to me to be too contrived, too 'loaded', to have been worth running this risk.

The winter of 1891–92, which had followed a season of disastrous harvests, threatened most of Russia with appalling famine. The government, far less efficient at providing relief than it was at censuring unfavourable opinions, was plainly unable to do enough for the starving peasantry. Chekhov had been seriously ill for many weeks—and like a lot of other doctors he was a bad patient, restless and resentful of being kept in bed—and as soon as he was out and about he became an ardent supporter of the various schemes for organizing private relief. Far too many of the peasants had lost all their horses, and Chekhov's own favourite relief plan was to buy a large number of animals, feed them until the snow had gone, and then distribute them in spring. He toiled away trying to raise, by all manner of means, a large public subscription, but the results were disappointing. He went as far as Nizhny Novgorod to see for himself how the famine relief was working, and braved snowstorms to visit the frozen villages. Feeling disheartened, he sharply declared there would be no famine round there if the people in Moscow and Petersburg did as much about the famine as they talked about it. He was driven back to Moscow by the threat of another illness. Later he went with Suvorin down to Voronezh, hoping to be given at once some sensible relief work to do. (In his medical capacity, Chekhov was an extremely hard-working practical man.) But the lordly Suvorin was not the right companion for such an expedition: he moved around in the wrong atmosphere. To his fury, Chekhov found himself attending heavy official dinners, not to his taste at any time and certainly unwelcome when surrounded by thousands of half-starved peasants. When allowed to escape from being a visiting celebrity, Chekhov did what he could, but after ten days went back to Moscow feeling he had been wasting time and energy.

Chekhov had now come to dislike Petersburg and its society. He was still fond of Moscow itself but found less and less to enjoy in his life there, rarely meeting people he wanted to meet, having his precious leisure frittered away by busybody acquaintances. What he wanted now was a place of his own, a house and something like an estate, in the country but not too remote. He could not afford to become a landowner—there would have to be more borrowing and on a large scale—but that is what he wanted to be, and soon he grew impatient. His motives were mixed and I doubt if he was fully aware of all of them himself. On a rational level he argued that living in the country cost less than it did in Moscow, that he would no longer have to rent summer places, that when the estate began to add to his income he would be free at last from any hack work, and that as a landowner, with a modest but well-organized estate, he would feel more confident about his future. But I suspect there were also two more or less hidden reasons. One grew out of the dissatisfaction he felt with his position as a writer, not in terms of popularity or literary prestige but of his own estimate of himself, his feeling that unless he soon attempted more original and more ambitious work he would be staring in secret at defeat. In short, I believe the future author of the great plays was urging him to move. Finally, I also believe that there was in Chekhov at this time a highly sensible, practical, organizing and creative kind of man trying to get out and show what he could do. This Chekhov, neither the writer nor the doctor, had felt bitterly frustrated during the muddle of the famine relief. So now he cried out for an opportunity —a country estate.

He was so impatient that he agreed to buy a house and estate before he had seen them. He had sent Masha and Mikhail to make a report, even though the whole place was deep under snow, and their vaguely favourable account set him in motion. Melikhovo, called after the neighbouring hamlet, was only a two-and-a-half hour railway journey from Moscow, though some miles from the nearest station. Chekhov and the family moved in before the snow was gone, and it was some weeks before they knew exactly what they had acquired. As the snow vanished, flower-beds, haystacks, a grove of lime trees appeared, a kind of fairy-play effect. But there were snags. The house was much smaller than Chekhov had hoped; the land, about 650 acres, was not good; everything around the place was dilapidated; the previous owner, an artist, had been an impudent liar; and Chekhov had already paid more than he had intended to pay and would have to keep on spending money. Trapped there in a house abounding with bedbugs, cockroaches, mice, saddled with a derelict farm, with a dreadful road between him and the nearest railway station, Chekhov might have given way to despair. He did not.

What we might call the Third Man in him, the practical, organizing, commanding man who had been awaiting his opportunity, took charge now. Money or no money, workers of every sort were brought in to repartition the house, to clean it and paint it and paper it, and give it some plumbing. All the sheds and fences and wells were put in good order. Chekhov himself planned and then supervised the building of a bathhouse, a barn, hothouses; enlarged the pond and stocked it with fish; and happily planted trees and flowers. His father was responsible for the estate paths, his mother for the house, Masha for the vegetable garden, Mikhail for field work—that is, when these two could come to Melikhovo, at week-ends and during vacations. Two farm labourers were employed, and, later, a cook and maid for the house, which was gradually enlarged to cope with all their summer visitors. The practical man joined with the artist in Chekhov to improve the place in every possible fashion. He had to do the work of three men, for he could not neglect his writing, nor his medicine, with all the sick peasants of the neighbourhood arriving for free treatment (and cholera was creeping in from the south, that first summer). Nevertheless, he could write to Suvorin: 'The kitchen garden is magnificent. There are perfect mountains of cucumbers and the cabbage is wonderful. If it were not for the accursed cholera I might say that I have never spent a summer so happily as this one.'

Venturing to oppose Professor Simmons again, I think it was not the years 1885–89 but the two or three springs and summers at Melikhovo that brought Chekhov the greatest happiness he ever knew. He loved the house and gardens and estate he had more

or less created himself. That all his friends should come in summer to enjoy them too delighted him. He was nearly always in the highest spirits at these times. Moreover, the practical creative man in him set to work beyond the boundaries of Melikhovo, to plan— to urge others to join him in building—new hospitals, schools, roads. But what about the *other* creative man in him, the writer, the artist? He was less on show than he had been before Melikhovo, but during the long hard winters, when he was not playing truant in Moscow or Petersburg, he worked steadily, perhaps at a deeper level than he had attempted before. It is true that not so many of his better or more ambitious stories date from these early 90s; but we do not know exactly how long he had worked on *The Seagull*, the first of his quartet of great plays, before he felt it was ready for production in 1896.

He was still in debt but he was gradually paying off his creditors. He was far less dependent now on quick sales of his stories to magazines. He had several books continuously in print and though the actual editions may have been small they succeeded one another steadily. And while he was no rival to a giant elder like Tolstoy (the two met at this time and took to each other at once), Chekhov now enjoyed the highest reputation among his contemporaries, with the result that stories of his were already being translated for publication, chiefly in reviews and magazines, throughout Western Europe. Freed from immediate worry about money, delighted to play the host at Melikhovo, his reputation growing steadily, Chekhov might have been entirely happy if he had known even moderately decent health. But the tuberculosis could not be checked. The coughing fits were often exhausting; he was beginning to suffer from intestinal troubles; and though he tried to pretend, perhaps even to himself, that there was nothing seriously wrong, the brutal facts had to be faced.

After much restless talk about travel to distant places (even to Chicago for its World Fair), early in 1894 Chekhov went to Yalta, a seaside resort in the Crimea to which many Russian doctors sent their consumptive patients. It may or may not have been good for his health; what is certain is that after the first two weeks or so he began to feel bored there. 'I am in Yalta,' he wrote to one of his favourite young women, 'and I am dreary, very dreary indeed.' He was soon to spend a great deal of his time in Yalta, the place most closely associated with him, where he wrote his two last and greatest plays, *The Three Sisters* and *The Cherry*

Anton Chekhov with his family and some friends near his house in Moscow (Novosti)

Anton Chekhov in Melikhovo, April 1897 (Novosti)

Orchard; but in his letters there is far more evidence that he disliked Yalta than there is that he ever really enjoyed staying there. It must have been—and indeed he declared it to be—a charming little town, but its invalidish, winter-resort atmosphere and style of life, beautifully suggested in *The Lady With The Dog*, bored or irritated him. It was not his kind of place. Its visitors were not his kind of people. He could find the company he liked best in Moscow and Petersburg, or among his guests at Melikhovo, to which he returned as soon as the worst of the winter was over.

It was not until 1899 that Chekhov finally decided to sell Melikhovo. But by this time he was not a man who could live where he pleased. Illness had aged him shockingly, and though he had returned to Melikhovo summer after summer, still filling it with guests, the old high spirits had almost vanished: this was a quiet wasted man looking at his roses. In 1897 he had tried a winter out of Russia, first staying at Biarritz, then moving to Nice, warmer and full of Russians, and finally remaining from March to May 1898, in Paris. His recent relations with Suvorin had not been good, chiefly because the luxurious Suvorin had shown no enthusiasm for Melikhovo. Now Chekhov's winter and spring in France led to a complete break between them, because Chekhov became an ardent supporter of Dreyfus and Zola, and Suvorin of course took the opposite official view. By 1899 early autumnal rains swept him out of Melikhovo; and now it had to be Yalta, where he bought land some miles out of the town, in a wildly romantic region, and began building, perhaps hoping to create a Crimean Melikhovo.

He could still draw plans and dream fine dreams, but now he was nearly forty and very different indeed from the eager and energetic man of thirty who had made up his mind to have an estate in the country. He abandoned his first scheme and settled into a villa in Yalta, an invalid surrounded by hundreds of other invalids, claiming his attention, asking for his help. What I feel were really his happiest days, the earlier summers at Melikhovo, all the long sunlit hours filled with work and play and friends, would soon be a fading memory. There is a kind of fragrance of regret haunting Chekhov's last plays, his masterpieces. Some of it perhaps came from the lost summers, the vanished rose-gardens, of Melikhovo.

Chapter 5

Anton Chekhov with the cast of the first production of 'The Seagull' *(Novosti)*

The Chekhov who settled reluctantly into that villa in Yalta was in effect a dying man. If he had been an ordinary man, not feeling passionately about anything, I doubt if he would have lasted a couple of years. Here I am not being sentimental. I do not think Chekhov was able to survive until the summer of 1904 because he fell in love and married at last. I believe in all seriousness that it was his genius, backed by an uncommonly strong will, that kept him alive. At last he was ready for the Theatre, and now, by the greatest good fortune, there was one company, the Moscow Art Theatre, ready for him. Certainly he was genuinely devoted to Olga Knipper, whom he married, but as one of its leading actresses she was a sort of warm and loving symbol of the Theatre that could at last do justice to his plays, so highly original, so subtle, so delicate and yet so strong. With the Moscow Art Theatre crying out for yet another play, and yet another, he had his work to do. So he kept alive until he did it. Every time he risked a visit to Moscow, liable to undo any little good that Yalta might have done, it was not simply to see Olga Knipper, though he was eager enough to do that, but even more, I believe, to get close to the beloved company happily engaged with his last play, anxious to begin rehearsing the next. These last few years, I feel, were dominated, shaped and coloured so far as his desperate situation allowed it, by the dramatist in him, not dying by inches like the man himself but living in the glow of a great sunset.

However, Chekhov was more or less ready before the Theatre was. He had finished his first version of *The Seagull* as early as 1895 and even had typewritten copies (rare at that time) for his friends to read. 'It is nothing special,' he wrote to one friend. 'In general, I'd say that I'm an indifferent dramatist.' This and similar offhand or deprecating references to the play and to himself as a dramatist suggest to me that he took *The Seagull* very seriously indeed and in it had already moved away from conventional playwriting. Not being sure how his new and highly original dramatic method would be received, he pretended—perhaps even to himself, to guard against disappointment—that the play was 'nothing special'. He risked reading it to a roomful of writers and theatre people in Moscow. Unfortunately most of his hearers were far less interested in his original method than they were in the fact that the Trigorin–Nina affair reminded them at once of a similar affair in their own circle. But Nemirovich-Danchenke, an intelligent theatre man, soon to create the Moscow Art Theatre with Stanislavsky, explained at length to Chekhov the play's dramatic weaknesses; and for once Chekhov, who could take criticism, listened in complete silence, not attempting to defend himself, to argue any point. Again, this unusual behaviour suggests to me that Chekhov had already decided which way he would go, and that not even a Nemirovich-Danchenko could turn him aside. As we discovered earlier, behind his light bantering manner, Chekhov had great force of character and will.

He revised *The Seagull*—but to what extent we do not know because his first draft vanished—and in the autumn of 1896 he agreed that the Alexandrinsky Theatre in Petersburg should produce it as a benefit performance for their most popular comedienne. For once Chekhov, in his eagerness to see his play on the stage, behaved quite stupidly. To begin with, a benefit audience would be largely composed of the comedienne's admirers, ready for a good laugh. Again, all the evidence suggested that the governing committee of the Alexandrinsky, together with its director and players, did not understand the play: they merely wanted his name on the bills. He attended a few rather perfunctory rehearsals, at which most of the players did not seem to know what they were doing. There was one exception, a young actress who took over the part of Nina at short notice. This was Vera Kommissarzhevskaya, afterwards a great star of the Russian Theatre. (Her younger brother came to London in the 1920s and did some brilliant Chekhov productions.) The actual performance was little better than the shambles of the rehearsals. The admirers of the comédienne, who was not acting that night herself but might well have been, began to get their laughs. The curtain of the first act was greeted with whistling and jeering. Chekhov endured another act and then fled to walk the streets. He was missing for hours, and when at last he returned to the Suvorins he said that if he lived to be seven hundred he would not give another play to the Theatre. For this he can be forgiven; he had suffered an appalling public humiliation. But the great dramatist stirring in him was ready if necessary to face other disasters.

So in spite of the Petersburg fiasco, Chekhov soon published the text of *The Seagull*. But now, in February 1897, he stayed in Moscow because he was deeply involved in an ambitious scheme to build a 'People's Palace', which would house a theatre, library, museum, lecture room, and so forth. Nothing came of the scheme but it was during its meetings that Chekhov ran into Stanislavsky. They did not take to each other. This is not surprising because Stanislavsky, a large, expansive but rather solemn type, completely failed to understand Chekhov's self-deprecating manner and laconic humour. They were to do great work together, yet I feel that to the very last, after intense collaboration, they never *quite* hit it off, never felt entirely at ease with each other. Even so, in order to follow Chekhov's career as a dramatist we must temporarily ignore him—leaving him to go abroad for his health—and turn our attention to Stanislavsky.

An actor and director himself, Stanislavsky had known and respected for years Chekhov's friend, Nemirovich-Danchenko, an experienced director and teacher of dramatic art. But they had never revealed to each other their discontents and ambitions. Then suddenly, in the summer of 1897, they really talked, never stopped for hours and hours and hours. Together they planned a new kind of theatrical company, of which Nemirovich-Danchenko would be the literary director, Stanislavsky the director of productions. Their players would not be casually employed; carefully selected and then given a long contract, all well-treated equally, they would have to be dedicated men and women, ready to work hard through lengthy rehearsals; no more slopping about half-drunk, ad-libbing and showing off. These two directors were not thinking about Chekhov then of course, while they were making their plans, but in fact they were busy banishing from their Theatre everything that up to now had disgusted Chekhov—the casual rehearsing, the improvising, the stale theatrical tricks, the false declaiming and attitudinizing. In creating this company they were beginning to move in the same direction, turning their back on the accepted Russian Theatre that Chekhov had already taken in his writing. So gradually, for there was a prodigious amount of work to be done, there came into existence what was finally called the Moscow Art Theatre.

Its creation was a great stroke of luck for Chekhov—and for us. Without it we might have had *Uncle Vanya*, based as it was on the earlier *Wood Demon*, but I doubt myself if we would have had *The Three Sisters* and *The Cherry Orchard* without the Moscow Art Theatre. His relations with it, though not always easy, came closer and closer to the centre of his being. It offered him the instruments, the only instruments, on which the music of his drama could be played. But not at first; all was doubtful at first, with the production of *The Seagull*. In *My Life In Art*, Stanislavsky, who directed the production and also played Trigorin, a testing part, describes the difficulties they faced. It took time to understand the play's 'inner line of action'; they had to press on with it because the company, in its opening season, was badly in need of a success; and Chekhov, confined to Yalta by a sudden relapse, would not be able to attend the final rehearsals. A disastrous first night like the one in Petersburg would be a dreadful, perhaps fatal, blow to the sick man; and his sister Masha tearfully begged the directors to postpone the first performance. But they were too deeply committed. *The Seagull* was the fourth production of this difficult opening season, which had not gone well. It would either save them or sink them. Before a rather thin house, it opened on 17 December 1898. The company was appallingly nervous. Olga Knipper, who was playing the important role of Arkadina the actress, was actually running a high temperature. When the curtain closed on the first act, not a sound came from the audience, the dismayed actors began creeping towards their dressing rooms, but then there came a gigantic roar, a wild demonstration of delight and admiration that would not allow the players, taking their calls, to leave the stage. The whole play had—and continued to have—a rapturous reception. It launched the Moscow Art Theatre on its great career. And from then on the curtains of the Theatre were decorated with a seagull, a perpetual tribute to Chekhov's triumph.

Having to remain in Yalta all winter, Chekhov felt restive and impatient, but he was kept busy answering all the telegrams and letters praising *The Seagull*. He was also involved in changing his publishers. Suvorin was not making sure his editors, distributors, book-keepers, were doing their work properly, and Chekhov had been dissatisfied with the firm for some time. A publisher called Marx offered to take over all Chekhov's work, buying it outright for an immediate lump sum, which was finally fixed at 75,000 roubles. Sister Masha, no fool, protested that this was far too little, which indeed it was, but then Chekhov was in need of ready money and had pushed Marx from 50,000 roubles to 75,000. He convinced himself—it is a favourite illusion of writers—that he was a keen hard bargainer, but he never convinced Masha. However, Marx could not claim any part of the royalties from plays, and, following the success of *The Seagull,* these began to trickle in. Chekhov worked hard collecting his stories for a definitive edition; he was also busy spending the money from Marx on various charities, public and private, and in building a villa in Yalta. Even so, he longed to be in Moscow and never really liked Yalta for itself, though at this time he did try to enliven the town. Among its visitors in early spring were two younger writers of unusual talent, Bunin and Gorky, admirers of Chekhov and soon to become his close friends.

Before he left Yalta for Moscow in the spring of 1899, Chekhov had already completely transformed his *Wood Demon* into *Uncle Vanya*. The directors of the Moscow Art Theatre were astonished and dismayed—as well they might be, after the triumph of *The Seagull*—to learn that Chekhov had offered *Uncle Vanya* to the Maly Theatre. (It was the oldest and most famous theatre in Russia, but that did not mean it would understand how to produce a Chekhov play. For once, Chekhov was behaving foolishly.) But before giving it to the Moscow Art Theatre, he pointed out that he had never seen their production of *The Seagull:* they must perform it for him. This was a most unreasonable request. The com-

Anton Chekhov's villa at Yalta (Novosti)

pany had finished their season; they had no theatre of their own yet; the scenery and costumes had been stored away; and a hastily improvised performance, in a strange theatre and without a proper audience, could not possibly do justice to their production. However, Chekhov insisted—and he was their great dramatist and a sick man—with the result that he sat with an audience of ten, showed no great joy, and severely criticized some of the per-formers, especially the actress playing Nina. In private he was severe too on Stanislavsky's Trigorin—more evidence of the lack of sympathy between them. But with one member of the company, the volatile and brilliant Olga Knipper, he had an increasingly close and affectionate relationship.

He attended the early rehearsals of *Uncle Vanya* that summer, giving the company's devoted young actors some excellent advice when they asked for it. But he had gone back to Yalta, hating his exile, some time before the final rehearsals and the opening night, which was at the end of October. There was a packed house, great excitement, much praise, but some reservations too: it was not *The Seagull* all over again. Chekhov tried to console Olga, who had written to say she had acted very badly (as Yelena, the professor's wife), by blaming himself, declaring that the play was old and already out of date; but he cannot have believed this; and indeed *Uncle Vanya* soon became—as it was to remain—one of the great triumphs of the Moscow Art Theatre. Though still at a maddening distance from the company, Chekhov was now falling almost as much in love with it as he was with Olga, and he promised to write a new play for them both. But he was needing more money than his play royalties were bringing him, and he began writing stories again. One of his little masterpieces, *The Lady With The Dog*, belongs to this period. Life in Yalta may have alternately bored and irritated him, but the first few pages of this story are a marvel of impressionism in writing.

Chekhov's letters from Yalta, especially those written to Olga Knipper, hard at work in Moscow with the Art Theatre, can easily give a wrong impression of his behaviour there. They tend to over-emphasize his boredom or irritation, showing a face that people in Yalta never saw. What they saw was the smiling helpful Dr Chekhov—though of course they knew he was a great writer too—who listened patiently to the appeals of his fellow invalids there, many of them in financial as well as physical distress. His own health went up and down: sometimes he had to stay in bed, at

others he could see people, move around, work in the garden of his new villa, where his mother, now a widow, joined him. His sister Masha spent the Christmas vacation of 1899 with him at Yalta. She was still teaching in Moscow, and she and Olga Knipper, close friends now, passed many a late night in intimate talk. Masha knew that Olga was deeply in love with her brother.

Olga and Chekhov had enjoyed a holiday together, in the South, the previous summer. Now in 1900, when there was much gossip about them in theatrical and literary circles, the question was: Would Chekhov make her his wife? The doubts and hesitations were on his side, not hers. He longed to be with her, that is quite clear from his letters, from his constant desire to leave Yalta for Moscow; but marriage was something else. Why tie a lively young woman to a man even older than his years and already an invalid, who could no longer live where he liked, go where he pleased? On the other hand, the fact that she was an actress, ambitious and passionately devoted to her profession, was in her favour. Even if they married, she would still have a rewarding life of her own and would not be drooping at his bedside. Olga herself was an extremely attractive person, no intellectual but quick and intelligent, and unlike so many successful actresses she could forget the Theatre when not working in it and could enjoy and talk eagerly about other things. Her nature was more ardent and demanding than his, and it is fairly certain—even though their more intimate correspondence is not available—that she was more deeply and passionately involved in their relationship than he was. But he wanted to be with her as he had never wanted before to be with any other woman.

He was too ill to leave Yalta while the winter of early 1900 still lingered, and in his letters he was wistful and yearning about being so far away from Olga and the Moscow Art Theatre. Why couldn't they come to Yalta? And this they decided to do, cancelling what might have been a lucrative engagement. (The theatre was still losing money, except with its two Chekhov plays. A little later it was taken over by the wealthy art-loving Morozov, who not only financed it but successfully reorganized it.) Stanislavsky risked the Crimean tour because he felt that if Chekhov saw *The Seagull* and *Uncle Vanya* properly produced, and with enthusiastic audiences, he would agree to write other plays for the company. Olga arrived first, with Masha, and there were excited plans and preparations to receive the company, which would play first in Sevastopol and

Anton Chekhov, 1900 (Novosti)

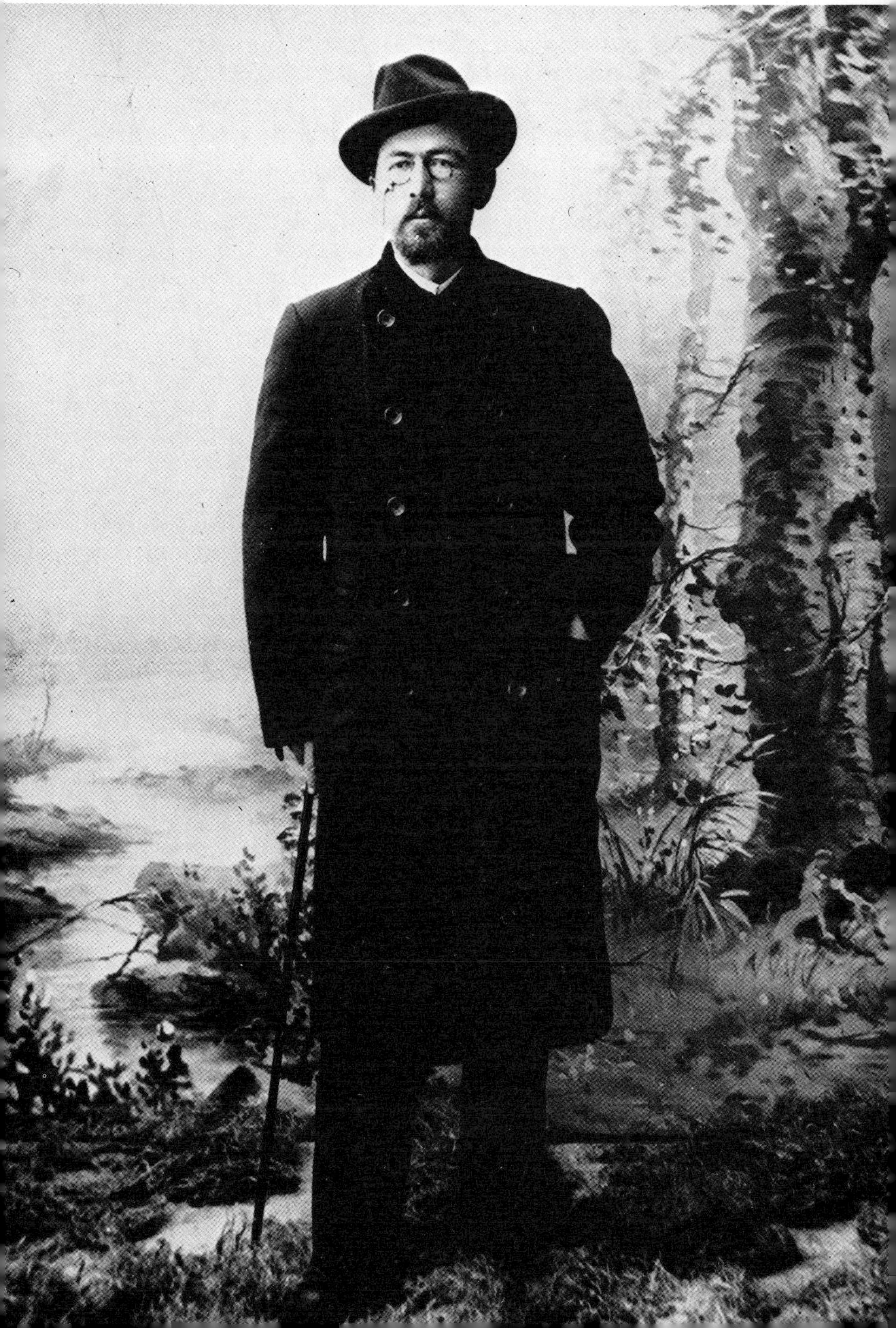

then in Yalta. Chekhov, who had been in the lowest of spirits for months, was now a changed man, as if the beautiful Crimean spring had transformed him too. Now he shared as best he could the rollicking high spirits of the young actors, who felt they were on holiday in an enchanting new country. He stayed in Sevastopol to share the Theatre's triumph there, and then during its ten days engagement in Yalta he played the happy and generous host, surrounded not only by the actors but also by many of his literary friends, who had gone specially to Yalta to celebrate this occasion. When Russians are happy and gay—and I am thinking now in terms of artists and not of politicians and bureaucrats—they are probably happier and gayer than anybody else.

Feeling restless and empty after the Moscow Art Theatre had gone, he tried a visit to Moscow but had to cut it short. He went with Gorky and other friends on a tour of the Caucasus. Olga, free of rehearsing for the next season, came to stay with the Chekhovs in July, and there is some evidence that while Anton and Olga were together here, his final reserves began to melt,so that their marriage now seemed to her inevitable. Stanislavsky was pressing him hard for the new play he had promised. Towards the end of summer he began writing it—the drama of three sisters—but found it difficult, having saddled himself with too many characters, and was maddened by having to entertain large numbers of long-winded visitors. Impatient to see him, Olga wrote letter after letter urging him to come to Moscow, but he felt he had to stick to his desk, even if for days he wrote nothing. He finished this first draft of the play by the middle of October, and braved the cold and damp of Moscow by going there himself. Stanislavsky arranged a reading of *The Three Sisters*, attended by the full company. It was followed by a bewildered silence; and then, after overhearing some foolish remarks among the young actors, Chekhov walked out, angry for once. However, he stayed on in Moscow, though every week was an added risk, and revised the first two acts, which were soon put into rehearsal. It was impossible for Chekhov to remain in mid-winter Moscow; he loathed the idea of returning to Yalta; so he went to Nice and finished the play, completely rewriting the fourth act, in the Russian *pension* there. At the same time he not only wrote frequently to Olga (who was having trouble with her part, Masha) but also to Stanislavsky and some of his actors, who needed advice. (Stanislavsky's account of this production in his *My Life In Art* is not quite accurate.) Above all, Chekhov insisted

48

Anton Chekhov and his wife, Olga Knipper-Chekhov (Novosti)

that the dress, bearing and manners of the officers in the play must be true to life.

Once again, he was not able to be present at the first night of one of his masterpieces. When *The Three Sisters* opened, on 31 January 1901, he had left Nice for Italy; the Moscow Art Theatre did not know where to send its telegrams. The play was not an immediate success, except with a few fellow writers who understood its depth, but it held its place in the Theatre's repertory and gradually became more widely appreciated. After running into cold weather in Italy. Chekhov went by sea to Odessa and then to Yalta. His boredom there was banished by Bunin, ten years younger and a man of great charm and talent, and a fervent admirer of Chekhov. (Both Bunin and Gorky, frequent visitors to Yalta, wrote valuable reminiscences of Chekhov at this period.) The Moscow Art Theatre went up to Petersburg, where Chekhov's plays had finely appreciative audiences but were slashed by the conservative Petersburg critics, to the great distress of Olga. Chekhov begged her to join him at Yalta as soon as this season was over, but at first she refused, making it plain that she felt it was time they married. She was now in the maddening situation of being continually asked by friends, his as well as hers, *when* it would be. Chekhov told Bunin he was going to get married, but though his letters to Olga were ardent enough he still did not offer her a time and place for their wedding. Chekhov, as we have seen, had never been a marrying man, and now, almost a physical wreck, knowing he had only a few years to live, he felt reluctant to bind himself to a young woman with an enormous zest for life. (I must add here that his tuberculosis itself was no barrier because in Russia then it was not generally regarded as being highly infectious.) Moreover, knowing how most women behave, he could easily imagine 'scenes' between Olga as wife and his rather possessive sister and mother. In the end, Olga did go to Yalta for a brief stay but left without any definite promise from Chekhov, as she reminded him somewhat bitterly after her return to Moscow. Then he gave in and said they would be married in Moscow sometime in May. He reminded her that he detested all ceremonies and social fuss, so it would have to be all done secretly. And it was, so that at first even his family did not know.

Before his marriage Chekhov had been thoroughly examined by a Moscow specialist, who told him either to go to Switzerland or to the distant Ufa province to try the koumiss treatment. (This consisted of drinking large quantities of koumiss, a time-old Tartar beverage, made out of fermented mares' milk, that was considered to have unusual medicinal properties.) So Anton and Olga Chekhov departed for a koumiss honeymoon, living in a remote and not very comfortable sanatorium in a forest. The forest was beautiful; the koumiss was doing him good; Olga was happy enough; but after a few weeks Chekhov was tired of the place and cut the treatment short. (The ravages of his disease now seemed to make Chekhov equally impatient with too much quiet and too much noise, bustle, entertaining.) They left for Yalta. Masha was on holiday in the villa with her mother, and they had already had letters from her that suggested she was considerably disturbed by the marriage. Chekhov must have wondered on the way there if he had been wise to leave the peace of the forest so soon.

As the name Knipper suggests, Olga's family background was not Russian but German. She might adore pleasure and gaiety but she liked order and thoroughness and was suspicious of sketchy Russian housekeeping. And she was now returning to the villa as its master's wife. He was a sick man and while she was under the same roof she alone must take care of him, decide what was best for him. As Chekhov must have known it would, this roused opposition in the equally possessive Masha. It was an uneasy time for a man who detested quarrels and scenes even more than most writers—and they in turn suffer more than most men from any lack of domestic harmony. Towards the end of August Olga went to Moscow to begin rehearsals, leaving behind her elaborate instructions for the care and comfort of her husband that may or may not have been followed by Masha and her mother. But Chekhov was now deeply devoted and emotionally committed to Olga; even a few weeks separation made him feel wretched; so he decided to go to Moscow, ostensibly to take a look at the final rehearsals of *The Three Sisters*, which was opening again on 21 September. (Though he himself often denied this, any stay in Moscow longer than a few days was now gravely damaging to his health. We have to bear this in mind.) There were many things in Stanislavsky's production he disliked and tried to put right. Dramatists and directors are rarely in complete agreement, and the modest humorous Chekhov, as Stanislavsky points out, could be quite ruthless about the casting and staging of his plays. Stanislavsky was a sensitive and meticulous director but he had almost a mania for introducing all manner of little sounds—that of a distant passing train, the soft strumming of a guitar, the cry of a bird, even the scratching of a mouse—not for greater naturalism but in order, so to speak, to 'orchestrate' the production; and Chekhov, who made effective use of pauses and sudden silences in his stage directions, greatly disliked this constant fuss in the ear and kept protesting against it. The slightly revised production of *The Three Sisters* was immediately successful, and Chekhov, who had to take a curtain call, was rapturously received.

He was now fascinated by the work of the Moscow Art Theatre and had an affection for most of the company. But it kept its leading actresses rehearsing all day and performing most nights, so Chekhov was seeing little of Olga, unless he chose to join her at the late-night parties to which she was always being invited. After four weeks in Moscow, feeling really ill again, he went to see the specialist, who ordered him to return to Yalta as soon as possible. He and Olga parted sadly. Olga, the healthy lively one, felt the enforced separation even more than he did, for he at least was weary and knew he needed rest and quiet. He was helped through the lonely winter by a long visit from Gorky and by the presence, only a few miles along the coast, of Tolstoy. They had met before and Chekhov had an enormous respect and admiration for Tolstoy the writer, while sharply criticizing Tolstoy the eccentric prophet. (Peasants should be brought up to the level of good writers, Chekhov declared, and good writers should not be forced down to the level of peasants.) Tolstoy thought Chekhov's plays were nonsense but greatly admired his stories and was very fond of him as a man. So Chekhov, sitting modestly silent, half-smiling, spent hours listening to the roaring old giant denouncing everything.

Various prizes and official honours came his way at this time. He refused to take them seriously, using them chiefly as material for jokes. Whatever he may have pretended, he suspected that he had only a few more years to live. (A local doctor was now in fairly constant attendance upon him.) The separation from Olga was bad for them both, an increasing strain. This probably heightened her greed for pleasure and a gay social life, but when Chekhov, sick and lonely in Yalta, learnt both from her and his sister Masha how she went night after night to splendid suppers, late-night parties, dances, he told her tenderly to enjoy herself so long as all this gaiety did not interfere with her work. He never suggested she should leave the Theatre to be with him. On the other hand, he

Anton Chekhov and Maxim Gorky 1900 (Novosti)

knew that all her plans for them to live together in or near Moscow were impossible until the end of spring. The Theatre would not let her go for Christmas, a bitter disappointment to him, but she did snatch a few days at Yalta in February. Then in the middle of April she arrived at last, but on a stretcher, as much an invalid as he was, for at the end of March she had had an unexpected miscarriage and for two weeks had been dangerously ill. Foolishly they left Yalta together in May for Moscow, where Olga suffered a serious relapse. By June she had recovered and Chekhov left her with her mother, having accepted an invitation from the wealthy Morozov to visit his estate in the Urals. Then they spent the rest of the summer together at an estate just outside Moscow, owned by Stanislavsky's mother. (Stanislavsky himself had been extraordinarily kind and attentive to both of them, so that at last Chekhov felt friendly towards him.) But when the time came in August for Olga to begin rehearsing again, Chekhov told her he must go back to Yalta. He must write just as she must act, and he could do this best at Yalta.

This decision of his brought them to the only really serious quarrel they had had so far, so serious that Olga was writing angrily to him at Yalta that they might as well separate. 'We are making a mess out of our life,' she raged. 'My God, if I only knew that you needed me, that I could help you live, that you would feel happy if I were always near you! If you could only give me that assurance!' It was the cry of a highly extraverted woman to a deeply introverted man, always a little elusive, however affectionate, guarding in secret the impressions, thoughts, emotions, that he wished to transform into art. Olga had known intuitively for some time that she was barred from his inner world. But then so was everybody else, though that would never pacify an eager devoted wife. There was a secretive element in Chekhov that was an essential part of him as an artist. In a society where so many people were declaiming and confessing all day and half the night, he kept silent or made little humorous remarks. Among writers who could not stop talking about the work they were doing or were about to do, he rarely said anything about what he was writing or planning to write. One charge Olga made against him, during this crisis, was that he was so restless, so soon weary of people and places, so often complaining of boredom. This was true, and advanced tuberculosis can explain most of it. But there was something else. Life was slipping away, and lately he had been

TOP: *The study in the house at Yalta* (Novosti)
BOTTOM: *Chekhov's bedroom in the house at Yalta* (Novosti)

writing little or nothing. Like so many of his characters, he could have cried in effect, 'We must work. We must work.'

It is true that when they were completely reconciled and were exchanging letters every day or so, actually it was Olga who kept urging him to get on with his work. Like many people, far from stupid about most things, she did not understand the creative process in its depths, she imagined that writing a great play was entirely a matter of will and energy. But Chekhov now had to husband his energy and not waste the little he had left, between spells of complete prostration, on anything that did not represent him at his best. Olga wanted another wonderful part; the Moscow Art Theatre implored him to give them a new play for its 1902–1903 season; and Chekhov was anxious enough to oblige the Theatre and delight his wife. But the 'comedy' to which he made many vague references would not shape itself properly. He turned to the short story again and in April 1902 published one of his little masterpieces, *The Bishop*. Another short story, his last, *The Betrothed*, took him months to write and then revise. He was now almost a physical wreck, beginning to look like an old man. Any account in detail of these last two years of his life would be wearisome and infinitely melancholy. Plans eagerly made had to be abandoned; visits to Moscow, with Olga there and the Theatre and so many literary friends, would be enjoyed at first but would end in exhaustion; sadly he would return to Yalta, which he had now begun to detest. Then, feeling rather better, he would happily announce he was ready to travel again—then Moscow once more and another collapse.

Chekhov's villa in Yalta, as a tribute to his memory, has been more or less preserved to look as it was when he lived there. It can be visited and I went through it myself some years ago. It is not as light and airy as it must have been in his time, chiefly because the trees he planted are tall and thick now. But there is something strongly reminiscent of Chekhov—and indeed rather moving—in its neat simplicity, in the absence of anything large and pretentious, in its clean good taste. And in one or two of the rooms, you feel that Chekhov might have just gone out to stroll along the sea front.

What hangs over these last two years of Chekhov's life—first a dark cloud, then a mist, then a burst of bright sunlight—is this 'comedy' he was brooding over and struggling with—now known throughout the world as *The Cherry Orchard*. He began it in the spring of 1903, when he and Olga were living near Moscow, and

Anton Chekhov on the balcony of his house at Yalta (*Novosti*)

completed it and then revised it in the autumn, when Olga had had to return to the Theatre and he was alone at Yalta. He was extremely weak, had no appetite, was exhausted by his coughing and a form of dysentery, and if and when he could work at all, it was often reduced to a few lines a day. It was not until well into October that the Theatre received the first draft of the play. Because he had worked so slowly and was beginning to wonder if his writing and judgment were failing—but perhaps too because somewhere at the back of his mind he believed that this would be his last play and might somehow be an original masterpiece—he felt intense anxiety about its reception by Nemirovich-Danchenko and Stanislavsky. Two highly enthusiastic telegrams partly re-assured him, but only partly because he felt intuitively that what he had written had not been fully understood. He was furious when an inaccurate and botched account of the play was given to a newspaper. He fired urgent letters at Olga and the two directors, giving them descriptions of the characters in the play and sug-gestions for casting them.

When he arrived in Moscow, early in December, to attend rehearsals, he declared he was feeling much better, though his friends, shocked by his ravaged looks, found this hard to believe. As he had anticipated, he was soon sharply disagreeing with Stanislavsky. He had always felt that Stanislavsky's productions, though technically brilliant, had been 'too weepy'. Now, with *The Cherry Orchard*, author and director found themselves at cross-purposes. Chekhov insisted, as he had done all along, that he had written a comedy, full of droll people and laughable scenes. Stanislavsky saw it as primarily a lament over the vanishing aristocracy and their style of life, stressing and dragging out everything melancholy, so that the brief fourth act, to Chekhov's disgust, went on and on for forty minutes. Both men had to com-promise, in order to keep the rehearsals going at all, so both felt dissatisfied and dubious. 'I expect no particular success,' Chekhov wrote to an old friend, 'the thing is going poorly.' Equally doubtful, Stanislavsky contrived that the first night, 17 January 1904 (Chekhov's forty-fourth birthday), would coincide with the twenty-fifth anniversary of his literary career. An elaborate celebration of this event, with Chekhov himself on the stage be-tween the third and fourth act, would make the audience feel warm towards its author even if they felt uncertain about his play. So poor Chekhov, who thoroughly disliked pompous official occasions,

58

had to stand there, attended by the full company and representatives of literature and drama and the press, wearily listening to exactly the kind of high-flown tributes he had so often mocked. Moreover, he must have been wondering what the audience, in spite of their obvious enthusiasm on his appearance, would make of the play after this vast pompous interval between its third and fourth acts. The production in fact was not very well received. It was now bitterly cold in Moscow and though Chekhov stayed on, meeting many friends and admirers at home, he rarely ventured out. But somehow or other, perhaps by Chekhov's going through the play with Stanislavsky, the production must have been given a lift and a sparkle, have been brought nearer to Chekhov's conception. Not long afterwards it was a great success with the more difficult Petersburg critics and audiences, and then took a high place in the Moscow Art Theatre repertory.

After two months in Moscow, Chekhov rather surprisingly decided to go back to Yalta. He had no creative writing in mind, but he had accepted some editorial work for a literary magazine, hoping to discover some good young writers, and reading manuscripts and entertaining visitors helped him to pass most of his better days. Though his doctors were now warning him against travel, plans for possible long summer tours abroad with Olga enticed and excited him. But—ironically enough, in view of his tremendous reputation—he was worried again about money. Masha had been right, after all: he ought to have had better terms from Marx. His friends were so indignant about the Marx contract that they were preparing to make a public appeal against it. However, Marx let him have some extra money and there were one or two other windfalls. Now he felt they could go abroad or discover and then buy the kind of house they wanted, somewhere just outside Moscow. But his health, which had not been too bad during the earlier Yalta weeks, now rapidly deteriorated. Early in May, according to plan, he set out eagerly but very shakily to join Olga in Moscow. He was making this familiar journey for the last time.

He had to go straight to bed and stay there. Olga called in her own German doctor, who found Chekhov in such pain that he gave him morphine injections. It was agreed that as soon as Chekhov was fit to travel at all, he and Olga should go to Berlin to consult a specialist there. (His Russian doctors complained afterwards that these peremptory Germans had never sought their

Portrait of Chekhov, by I. Bras, in Tretyakov Gallery, Moscow (Novosti Press Agency)

advice and had behaved with fatal obstinacy.) During these final weeks in Moscow, the friends who called, finding him in a dressing gown, lying on a divan in his study, felt strongly they were seeing him for the last time. Even now, travel under pleasant conditions was so exciting that Chekhov felt much better at once, writing lively accounts of Berlin to his sister. Even in June, when he and Olga were settled in Badenweiler, a small spa near the Black Forest to which the specialist had sent them, he could write to Masha: 'We shall perhaps return to Yalta by sea from Trieste or some other port. Health is coming back to me, not by ounces but by stones . . . Oh, how badly the German women dress!' But he began to dislike the place and complained of the heat. Towards the end of June he suffered a heart attack and had to be given morphine and oxygen. On 1 July he said he felt so much better that in the evening he begged Olga to leave his bedside and take a walk in the park. When she returned, he was even able to improvise a comic story for her. But after midnight he came out of his sleep to ask her—for the very first time in their life together—to summon a doctor. It was an hour and a half before the doctor arrived, and as soon as he approached the bed Chekhov clearly announced his own dissolution, saying *Ich sterbe*. He allowed the doctor to give him an injection of camphor but refused oxygen, declaring that before it could be brought he would be a corpse. But he accepted a glass of champagne from a bottle the doctor ordered. He turned to Olga, gave her one of his enchanting smiles, said, 'It is some time since I have drunk champagne', slowly emptied the glass, lay down on his side, and never spoke again. When the dawn crept in, with all the birdsong from the garden, the unmoving face still wore a smile.

That is how Anton Chekhov, aged forty-four, died in the early hours 2 July 1904. But it was as if he were still improvising stories, from somewhere behind the veil. So for example, after the doctor had left her alone with her dead husband, Olga saw a large black moth flutter in through the open window and then begin dashing itself against the lamp and the walls. Next she was startled by an odd explosion: the cork had been blown out of the champagne bottle. Then the moth found its way back to the night. The death-bed, the black moth, the champagne bottle firing its cork—they might have been brought together in one of Chekhov's shorter tales. As for his own funeral, in Moscow, Chekhov might have created the whole thing in one of his half-sardonic, half-farcical moods. The coffin came to the Moscow station in a van plainly

Anton Chekhov's funeral cortège, Moscow 1904 *(Novosti)*

labelled *Oysters*. There was great confusion in and around the station. A military band started playing and then went marching off, and some of Chekhov's mourners joined the procession, though in fact the coffin they were marching behind belonged to a general who had been killed in the Russo-Japanese War. Walking together in the real procession, and already in a fury after so much confusion, Gorky and Chaliapine angrily overheard exactly the kind of complacent banalities Chekhov mocked in his stories. When the procession stopped in front of the Moscow Art Theatre, the Chekhov family were waiting to join it but were having a lot of trouble proving who they were. On the way to the monastery, the crowd grew enormously; there was a lot of scuffling at the narrow entrance; for some time the pallbearers and chief mourners could not get into the cemetery, which was soon half-wrecked by an impatient shouting mob, leaving behind them broken fences, cracked headstones, scattered trodden flowers. Angrier than ever now, crying and cursing, Chaliapine shouted to Gorky, 'That's the scum he lived and worked for and tried to teach!' It might have been a Chekhov story called *The Funeral*. Perhaps it was.

Chapter 6

The study in Chekhov's house in Moscow (*Novosti*)

Chekhov's more important stories have long been known and admired in all civilized countries. It is he more than any other writer who has been responsible for the literary vogue of the short-story form, very much in fashion during the 1920s both in Britain and America, where many anthologies of short stories appeared, together with much criticism of this particular form. (America had its professors of short-story writing.) Chekhov's influence has been immense, and has not ceased working even today. Nevertheless, I think it is safe to add that the astonishingly wide popularity of his stories in Russia has never been repeated elsewhere, and that his world stature as a writer is based not on his stories but on his plays. Most of us think of him first as a dramatist.

Here I must make a confession. Though I hope—and indeed believe—I can fully appreciate Chekhov's little masterpieces, I must admit I have long had a certain prejudice against the short story itself. I would rather read one good novel, especially if it is a substantial work, than a dozen short stories, however good they may be. This has nothing to do with the art of the writer. My complaint against the *literary* short story, as distinguished from highly artificial tales with trick endings, is that it tends to falsify life. The writer may be trying to be absolutely honest but he is so dangerously restricted by the form that he over-simplifies his people and their destinies. Chekhov can often be discovered doing just this, especially during the middle period of his story-telling, roughly 1885 to 1895. Too many of his leading characters are compelled to suffer from the 'Now-life-is-all-over' syndrome. And life, in its richness, its variety, its surprising twists and turns, might very well *not* be all over if it were not being squeezed into the short-story form. Much of Chekhov's reputation as a gloomy writer, a confirmed pessimist, comes from the limitations of the form he chose, its frequent demands for a 'Life-is-over' climax. This must not be confused with his own peculiar atmosphere of tender melancholy that pervades his best stories and his plays.

'You complain,' he wrote to a woman friend in 1897, 'that my heroes are gloomy—alas! that's not my fault. This happens apart from my will, and when I write it does not seem to me that I am writing gloomily; in any case, as I work I am always in excellent spirits . . .' But then by 1897 he had been sharply reacting for years against the kind of fiction this friend most enjoyed. Once he had freed himself from hasty little hack jobs for the cheap magazines —and even from these he must have learnt the virtue of brevity, of economy—he turned his back on other writers (except when he came under Tolstoy's influence for a time) and went his own way.

However, before considering how he went his own way, we can take a quick look at two different lines of negative criticism. Along one of them he was accused of being too cold, too much the detached observer, the doctor in his surgery. I believe this to be quite wrong. The deep compassion was always there, but he had his own method of awakening it in the reader. 'When you depict sad or unlucky people,' he wrote to a younger writer, 'and want to touch the reader's heart, try to be colder—it gives their grief, as it were, a background, against which it stands out in greater relief. As it is, your heroes weep and you sigh. Yes, you must be cold.' Again, after praising some early stories of Gorky, he could not help adding: '. . . To my mind you have not enough restraint. You are like a spectator at the theatre who expresses his transports with so little restraint that he prevents himself and other people from listening.' It is Chekhov's own restraint, his 'coldness', that arouses our own compassion for his 'sad or unlucky people'. He knew exactly what he was doing.

The second line of negative criticism takes us away from his contemporary Russian readers. Indeed, I shall make it quite personal. I shall begin by admitting that during the 1880s and 1890s Russia was an unhappy country. The aristocratic land-owning system was breaking down; the reformers—to say nothing of the revolutionaries—could make little progress; outside its few large cities it was appallingly backward when compared with Western Europe; and the kind of small provincial town, fifty miles from anywhere, that Chekhov so often describes was no doubt dismally banal, corrupt, stupid, on one level and ignorant, drunken, brutal, on the level below. Moreover, such towns would always have a few members of the *intelligentsia* defeated by their environment, permanently frustrated, weak-willed, for ever talking and drinking and never attempting anything constructive. (It is a very familiar Chekhov type.) Having admitted so much, I shall venture to say that Chekhov does seem to me to overload some of his stories with misery and despair. Take for example one of his longer stories, *Ward No. 6*, in which the good-hearted but ineffectual Dr. Ragin is declared a lunatic, shut away in the mental ward of his own hospital, and there mercilessly beaten until released by death. This story had a sensational reception and was enormously admired by the more liberal critics. Yet I for one cannot help feeling that it would have been a much better story—and more convincing to us here and now—if Chekhov himself had been more restrained. There is too much ignorance, stupidity, brutality and wickedness: the dice are too heavily loaded against poor Dr. Ragin. We are not even in Russia's worst town: we are in hell.

Chekhov was not a novelist and his longer and more ambitious stories rarely show him at his best. *The Duel*, for instance, which was published as a separate volume after being serialized, has some fine things in it—the behaviour and talk of the women, the picnic, the duel itself—but the tirades and lectures of the zoologist, Von Koren, and the depravity and sudden reformation of Laevsky are not good Chekhov. *An Anonymous Story* is not without interest if only because of its unusual Petersburg background and types, and Zina, the mistress, is superbly drawn, but the story as a whole leaves us suspicious and dissatisfied. *A Woman's Kingdom*, written in 1894 when he was to some extent influenced by Tolstoy, might almost be socialist-realist propaganda, not our Chekhov. *In the Ravine,* much admired by Tolstoy, is a powerful study of a remote community of peasants and small shopkeepers, but I think I would have found it more effective if it had been either shorter or longer. Oddly enough, what is perhaps the most rewarding, the most haunting, of his lengthy pieces is also the earliest but one of them, *The Steppe,* written in 1888. But then it is not really a story at all but a kind of prose poem. The earliest of all and often published separately as a short novel is *The Shooting Party,* written in 1885, and excluded by Chekhov himself from his collected works. It is readable but well below the later Chekhov standard.

The range of the shorter stories, as distinct from the *novellas* mentioned above, is astounding, with at one extreme the sardonic little tales, with an ironic twist in them, like *A Transgression* and *Chorus Girl,* and at the other the late masterpieces like *The Lady With The Dog, The Darling,* and *The Bishop,* which also are comparatively short but offer us a marvellous, a magical, distillation of life. I have already pointed how broadly-based Chekhov was as a story-teller, his own personal experience having been so wide. It is true he keeps away from the highest circles of aristocratic, political, military life, not necessarily because he was not acquainted with its personages but, I imagine, because stories involving them, realistically in Chekhov's manner, would never have passed the censors. It is also true he tends to avoid very successful, supremely self-confident characters. He is happiest with peasants of all kinds, shopkeepers and minor officials, small-town schoolteachers and doctors, and all manner of posturing, ineffectual, neurotic intellectuals, characteristic of his Russia of the 1880s and 1890s. And for all of these, a huge variety, he has a wonderful eye and ear.

Let me offer one example out of hundreds. The sick old bishop, in the story with that name, had to endure a session lasting about an hour, with a wealthy young merchant, who had some grievance, talked very loudly, almost shouted, and was difficult to understand. 'God grant it may,' the young merchant said as he went away. 'Most essential! According to circumstances, your holiness! I trust it may.' Now to my mind the whole of that tedious wearing interview is perfectly suggested by those final absurd remarks. Chekhov has a genius—and it *is* genius, not simply an experienced writer's trick—for this power of suggestion, this maximum of effect created by the smallest possible means. (And here his influence on later writers throughout the world has been all to the good.) He can do it with people, with situations, with backgrounds. He could do more with fifty words than most of his contemporaries could do with five hundred. He is the master in language of the swift impressionistic sketch or the powerful drawing with most of the lines left out.

Admittedly he was not as drastically laconic as his talk might suggest. His famous pronouncement that a writer need not describe the moonlight, only the glint of it in a broken bottle, need not be taken too seriously: his own practice was rarely so economical. Talking to Bunin once on the shore at Yalta, Chekhov said, 'It is very difficult to describe the sea. Do you know the description of it that I read in the copybook of a schoolboy not long ago? *The sea was huge.* Only that. I think it is beautiful.' There is some playfulness here. Even so, by insisting on brevity, by concentrating on a few essentials of a scene or a character, he awakens and then satisfies our imagination by enticing it to cooperate with him. He himself was a hard worker, but as a writer he never makes us feel that he is working too hard, trying to take our sympathy by storm.

'I think that in Anton Chekhov's presence,' Gorky tells us, 'every one involuntarily felt in himself a desire to be simpler, more truthful, more oneself . . .' But his presence could not be everywhere, so he wrote stories, in which he held up to the face of Russia a clear mirror. He wrote in his notebook, 'Man will only become better when you make him see what he is like'; and again, but narrowing the issue, 'The power and salvation of a people lie in its intelligentsia, in the intellectuals who think honestly, feel, and can work.' So his sharpest character-drawing was reserved for intellectuals who refused to think honestly, who paraded their sensitiveness but at heart were unfeeling, who talked and talked but did no work. (And we have seen how, at every stage of his career, he worked with a will and strong sense of purpose.) Yet, with the exception of a few pages, there is in the stories written in his maturity no trace of that venom found in many satirists, who arrive snarling to revenge themselves. There can be no doubt—and his notebooks confirm this—that the Russia of his time, so sprawling, lazy, muddled, appalled him. Yet he loved it, could not be happy long away from it. There is always in the background, rising like an autumn mist to hide at last the ugliest features of the scene, his unwearying compassion, without which he could never have achieved, either as storyteller or dramatist, that intensely personal 'laughter-through-tears' effect we associate with him.

Among his *Themes, Thoughts, Notes,* we find this. 'Essentially,' he begins, 'all this is crude and meaningless, and romantic love appears as meaningless as an avalanche which involuntarily rolls down a mountain and overwhelms people. But when one listens to music, all this is—that some people lie in their graves and sleep, and that one woman is alive and, grey-haired, is now sitting in a box in the theatre, seems quiet and majestic, and the avalanche no longer meaningless, since in nature everything has a meaning. And everything is forgiven, and it would be strange not to forgive.' It seems to me that when we read the best of Chekhov we always catch the sound of something, faint and faraway and yet somehow always rising above the creaking of carts, the galloping horses, the din in the taverns, the loud chatter of the drawing rooms: it is that music which tells us that everything is forgiven and that it would be strange not to forgive.

Chapter 7

A scene from the first production of 'The Three Sisters' (Novosti)

The first Chekhov play I ever saw was *The Cherry Orchard*. This was in 1925 when it had its first London run. (There had been a single Stage Society performance as far back as 1911.) I took a girl with me, an intelligent girl who was a newly qualified doctor, and I remember that she left the theatre feeling bewildered and rather resentful. But the play, even in this faulty production, had enchanted me. The magic of it lingered for days. Since then I have seen many different productions of *The Cherry Orchard*. The best I ever saw was when I was in Russia in 1945, in a performance beginning at the curious hour of noon on Sunday, and it was of course being given by the Moscow Art Theatre, largely by players who had been trained and directed by Stanislavsky. Compared with that, the performance given by the Moscow Art Theatre during its visit to London in 1958 was disappointing. Incidentally, almost all the earlier British and American productions of Chekhov were too slow, heavy, lugubrious, missing the shot-silk 'laughter-

Two scenes from the Royal Shakespeare Company's 1961 production of 'The Cherry Orchard', with Peggy Ashcroft and John Gielgud (Angus McBean)

through-tears' effect. Chekhov himself would have detested them.

After so many years I do not remember what my girl-doctor companion said after we left the theatre that evening in 1925. But it is a fairly safe guess to suppose she told me that 'nothing happened'. It was a common complaint for some time against Chekhov and his four last plays. In point of fact a great deal happens in these plays, and indeed in *The Seagull, Uncle Vanya* and *The Three Sisters* there are moments that might have come from melodrama. It is not the dramatic substance of these plays that used to leave audiences feeling bewildered and dissatisfied: it is Chekhov's peculiar method. What he does in effect is to turn the conventional 'well-made' play upside down and inside out. It is almost as if he had read some textbooks on the art of playwriting and had then done the opposite of everything they recommended. It is common form in conventional drama to endow the leading characters, if only for the sake of the inevitable 'conflict', with more power of will and sense of purpose than most of us can pretend to have. Chekhov reverses this. Instead of heightening and hardening the will in his characters, he depresses and softens it: most of them are even more uncertain and weaker than we are. Again, in the 'well-made' play, the characters are so intent upon shaping neat scenes, are so anxious to reach the climax of the conflict, they cannot find time to tell us they dislike tomato soup or have an old uncle who still plays the 'cello. But if they are Chekhov characters, then they have time to tell us anything that comes into their heads.

There is a fascinating thing here that has escaped general notice. Chekhov himself, following some secret train of thought, was always surprising other people by making inconsequential remarks, just like so many characters in his plays. The others might be arguing about Marxism and he would say, 'Have you ever been to a stud farm?' Or the subject might be literature, and he would announce out of the blue, 'One ought to go to Australia.' Stanislavsky describes how Chekhov, a devoted angler, when he was out fishing with some theatrical friends, suddenly burst out laughing, and when they asked him what was the matter, he replied, 'Listen! Artem can never play Ibsen.' But what was a little idiosyncrasy in his own talk was broadened and deepened to become a highly original method in his drama. It enables us to come closer to his characters. It reminds us how difficult true communication can be. (Act Two of *The Cherry Orchard* originally ended with a scene between Charlotta, the eccentric governess, and Firs, the very old

valet, who tried—entirely in vain—to explain their lives to each other. But it was decided during rehearsal to shorten the act and this scene had to go—most unfortunately, in my opinion.) This method also reminds us how essentially lonely we are, most of our time. Finally, it gives Chekhov's drama, on the surface so lackadaisical and inconsequential, rhythm and development in depth.

It is this depth, where consciousness dissolves into the fathomless unconscious, where new half-realized meanings gleam and then vanish like fish in some deep lake, that constantly renews for us the fascination of his drama. He can be disliked—anybody and any-thing can be disliked—but if we like him at all, then we can take his plays over and over again. I have seen dreadful productions of Chekhov, who makes demands that too many companies cannot meet, but even during the worst of them something of the magic has remained. He has, so to speak, an extra dimension. Many of his friends, while they loved him for his unfailing kindness, generosity and charm, found something teasingly elusive in his personality. He can be equally elusive in his plays. What is farcical turns into pathos, comedy dissolves into tragedy, while this in turn reveals a glint of irony. Let us take, as an obvious example, all those speeches about life being wonderful sometime in the future. As we hear or read those speeches we can almost see an enigmatic smile hovering above them. Whatever else Chekhov may be doing, he is not seizing an opportunity to declare his faith in progress. (But I am not saying he had no such faith, only that he was not writing plays to prove it.) Any attempt to saddle him, as a dramatist, with a political-economic-social purpose seems to me quite wrong. He goes to work on a deeper level.

Like many of his tales, his plays make us movingly aware of waste and loss. With the exception of his lovable old innocents, his characters, though they may suffer from self-deception and weak-ness of will, make us feel that Time has cheated them. It is as if Anton Chekhov, as distinct from the practical sensible Dr A. P. Chekhov, felt strongly when in a creative mood that there is some secret, which might reveal a very different scheme of things, that we have lost. There is a curious speech by Vershinin in *The Three Sisters*, beginning: 'I often say to myself: suppose one could start one's life over again, but this time with full knowledge? Suppose one could live one's life as one writes a school composition, once in rough draft, and then live it again in a fair copy?' It is worth noticing that although there is a great deal about love in these four plays, not one of them offers us an example of a happy lasting sexual relationship. And there is a significant entry in one of his notebooks: 'Love is either the residue of something that is degenerating and that was once tremendous or else a part of something that will become tremendous in the future. But in the present it cannot satisfy, it offers much less than is expected of it.' He may have had in mind the heady false romanticism common enough in the Russia he knew. But his conclusion—'it offers much less than is expected of it'—is oddly prophetic to us now, when among so much uncertainty, fear, hidden despair, sex is being asked to carry too heavy a load.

However, it is time to take a seat in the theatre and look at the plays themselves. From here on it must be understood that my criticism is very personal, an expression of my own likes and dislikes; it could not be anything else and remain honest; but at least I can add that I have seen many productions of these plays, including some in Moscow itself, and that my own theatrical experience has been very considerable. In any order of all-round merit, I would say that the last of these plays, *The Cherry Orchard*, comes first; then, a little below it, *The Three Sisters* (often called simply *Three Sisters*, but this sounds a bit brutal in English); and then, some way below and both on the same level, *Uncle Vanya* and *The Seagull*.

We have seen already how immensely popular *The Seagull* became as soon as it was produced by the Moscow Art Theatre. It is far closer to conventional drama than Chekhov's later plays. It is nothing like so subtle and elusive. Its characters create definite 'scenes'. And it offers us actresses and authors—incidentally, the last we shall see in Chekhov. Nor is it surprising that the first act should have been so rapturously received at its opening performance. It is a wonderful first act, strikingly original, and broad, rich and deep. I could enjoy seeing it again and then leaving the theatre. Not that the rest of the play is bad—far from it—but it has weaknesses more obvious as the play develops. One of them is that it has too large a circle of unrequited lovers: the A loves B, B loves C, C loves D pattern soon becomes irritating. Then Trigorin and Treplev are hard to accept. What Chekhov did here was to divide his own personality into three: Trigorin being the popular storyteller self he was getting tired of, Treplev being the self struggling with new forms of expression, and Dr

Two scenes from BBC's 1966 production of 'The Seagull' with Pamela Brown, Robert Stephens, Charles Carson and Robin Phillips (BBC)

Two scenes from BBC's 1966 production of 'The Seagull' with Pamela Brown, Robert Stephens, Charles Carson and Robin Phillips (BBC)

Dorn being his doctor-self, significantly sympathetic to Treplev's efforts. None of them quite succeeds as a separate creation, an independent character. Trigorin, a part notoriously difficult for actors, is presented as a weak, shallow, fashionable author, yet he shows an all-consuming devotion to his art that is neither weak nor shallow and would set him apart from fashionable hacks. (He says some very good things of course, but are they in character—and which character?) Again, unless I have been deceived about Treplev as a highly original young writer, then I cannot accept his suicide. Finally, though this is a minor criticism, Dr Dorn seems to carry weight that he never really uses. The women, especially Nina, are good acting parts but hardly memorable characters. The play itself is fine theatre, which explains its popularity, but even so I am now ready to leave after that wonderful first act.

I am happy to announce that the production of *Uncle Vanya* I most enjoyed was an English one, that by the Old Vic in 1945, with Richardson as Uncle Vanya, Olivier as Astrov, Joyce Redman as Sonya, Margaret Leighton as Yelena. Even though it has the advantage of a very moving last act, *Uncle Vanya* is not an easy play for an English-speaking audience to accept. Its main theme—that old Professor Serebryakov and his beautiful young wife, Yelena, are not worth the sacrifices that Uncle Vanya and Sonya have been making for them—is straightforward enough. But the Professor's social importance is not obvious to us, and we could do with a little more of him. The over-excitable Uncle Vanya, very much a Slav type, is always in danger of appearing quite farcical, and the scene in which he fires at—and misses—the Professor has always seemed to me, as people say, 'a bit much'. As we know, this play is based on a much earlier one, *The Wood Demon*. It was completed, probably rather hastily, in 1896, but there is some evidence that Chekhov may have worked on it as early as 1890. Certainly if he had been still revising it by the time he was writing *The Three Sisters* and was now at ease with his own method, the rather awkward soliloquies in *Uncle Vanya* would have been taken out, and, for example, Dr Astrov would have been less obviously explicit about his forests and the waste of the countryside. The old underlying theme of waste and loss is here again, but this play may be taken as a symbolic presentation of the Russia of the 1890s, when so many glittering empty types like the Professor and his wife were being maintained by the long hard work and the drastic economies of the Uncle Vanyas and the Sonyas—who

Two scenes from the Old Vic Theatre Company's 1945 production of 'Uncle Vanya' with Sybil Thorndike, Laurence Olivier, Ralph Richardson and George Relph (John Vickers)

must 'live through a long, long chain of days and weary evenings' and know no rest this side of the grave, only in Heaven.

There are some great plays that offer more to the imaginative reader than they do to the playgoer. (After seeing many productions of *King Lear* and *Antony and Cleopatra*, I think they are best enjoyed at home.) Chekhov's *The Three Sisters* is not one of these plays. So long as the production is worthy of it—and it is a difficult play to stage—it must be seen to be fully appreciated. I have described already how Chekhov took endless trouble over this play, constantly sending on textual revisions and advice to actors after he had been compelled to go abroad. The best production of it I ever saw was at the Moscow Art Theatre in 1945, with Tarasova, a magnificent actress, playing Olga Knipper's original part, Masha. (My only reservation about this production, superb in every detail, is that because it tried to keep together as many as possible of the players trained by Stanislavsky, the cast as a whole tended to be much older than the characters they were playing.) The first act, in which we have to be introduced to so many people, is rather awkward, and the opening scene, between the three sisters, offers us too much obvious exposition. On the other hand, the play gains in force and depth as it goes along, and the last act—properly produced and using a big stage—is overwhelming. There is no better example of Chekhov's unique 'laughter-through-tears' effect than the scene in which the little teacher, Kuligin, puts on the false beard in a pathetic attempt to amuse his wife and her two sisters. There is much irony in the play as well as great pathos, as one illusion after another fails the test of reality; but it is not intended as a complicated proof of human futility. While Anton Chekhov tenderly removes each illusion, Dr A. P. Chekhov is suggesting we should not waste the life we have by allowing idle dreams to rob it of colour, flavour and zest.

We have seen already how Chekhov found *The Cherry Orchard* hard to compose—and it *was* composed rather than written, almost like another *Das Lied von der Erde*. And not simply because he was then a very sick man, working under a sentence of death. But I think this influenced him to a degree beyond his conscious appreciation, so that while he protested over and over again that he was writing—or had written—a comedy, he was not aware how much sadness was seeping through. (Stanislavsky must have felt this, so that he was not really at cross-purposes with Chekhov, though he may have wanted to make too much of the dying-aristocracy theme.) But Chekhov must have found his 'comedy' hard to compose because it carried his unique dramatic method as far as it would go, while at the same time he had to handle a large and varied group of characters. Furthermore, he gave each act its own particular atmosphere: first, the waiting up in the dark hours and then the arrival at dawn; secondly, the revealing talk in the immense calm early evening; thirdly, the semi-hysterical atmosphere of the late party; and finally the hurried tearful departure from the desolate house. All four are wonderful in their own way, but to my mind the masterpiece is Act One, which has long seemed to me the finest single act in the whole of modern drama. Technically it is a marvel, but over and above what can be analysed it has a peculiar magic that is renewed year after year.

Too much can be made of the cherry orchard itself. It gave Chekhov a beautiful image for his title, and the sale of it helps to shape the drama. But it is the house and not the orchard that is the centre and heart of the play. All the characters—even Lopahin, who begins by telling us so—are intimately connected with the house. But this is not a play about closing a house or selling an orchard. What then is it 'about'? It is about time and change and folly and regret and vanished happiness and hope for the future. A little girl I once knew, quiet for once and sitting in a corner, was asked what was the matter, and replied: 'Life in this world'. *The Cherry Orchard* is about life in this world. Coldly considered, its characters are far from being admirable: Madame Ranevsky is a foolish woman only too anxious to return to a worthless young lover; Gaev is an amiable ass who talks too much; Anya is a goose and her Trofimov a solemn windbag; Lopahin, the practical self-made man, is confused and unhappy; Epihodov a clumsy idiot; Dunyasha a foolish girl; Yasha an insufferable jumped-up lad; and Firs far gone in senility. But Chekhov, who knows all this better than we do, is not coldly considering these people. Even more, I suspect, than we are consciously aware of, he is revealing them to us in a strange light, infinitely tender and compassionate, that might illuminate a man's mind when he is in effect saying farewell to this life. Chekhov talked vaguely about another play he was planning to write, but I think he never meant this seriously. He had already said goodbye in *The Cherry Orchard*, his masterpiece.

A final point about Chekhov as dramatist. He came to have an enormous influence upon younger writers. Now a man may be a magnificent dramatist himself and yet be a bad influence. This, in my opinion, is true of Shaw, who, out of his unusual temperament, experience, witty ebullience, was able to create unique comedies of debate. He is an easy man to enjoy and a very difficult man to follow, with the result that we have had far too many mediocre comedies, loud with argument, written under his influence. The opposite is true of Chekhov. Since his time we have had many Chekhovian plays. None of them rivals *The Cherry Orchard* or *The Three Sisters*, but they are not worse plays because of his influence, they are all better than they might have been. While appearing at first so indifferent to the immediate demands of the Theatre, in the end Chekhov liberated and enriched it.

The Chekhov memorial in the grounds of the hospital in which Chekhov worked, in Zvenigorod
(Novosti)

Chapter 8

(*Novosti*)

In order to do justice to Chekhov's unique quality as an all-round human being, I shall risk being thought fanciful. More than once, thinking about him, I have felt that he might have been a model for a new kind of man that our century badly needed (and —alas—has failed to produce). Consider what was combined in him. His training and outlook were scientific; he took his medicine very seriously, and to the last described himself as a doctor. But he was no theorist, no dogmatist, of science, and was entirely lacking in that arrogance which so often invades lecture rooms and laboratories. What he did—and he did a vast amount more than I have been able to report here—was essentially practical, immediately helpful to people he wanted to see in cleaner and brighter surroundings, people who might soon be healthier and happier. Unlike most Russian intellectuals, he refused to accept any ideologies. He was suspicious of systems dealing largely in elaborate abstractions: he was at once pragmatic and sceptical. Russian drawing rooms were full of people who were neither, who were unpractical and over-credulous. It was the same with religion and faith; so he could write, 'Between "There is a God" and "There is no God" lies a great expanse which the sincere sage traverses with much difficulty. The Russian knows only one of these two extremes, for the middle ground between them does not interest him. Hence, he usually knows nothing or very little.'

Yet this same Dr A. P. Chekhov, so practical, so sensible, so clear-sighted, so deeply convinced that science could rescue men from ignorance, sloth, brutality and suffering, was also Anton Chekhov the writer. Doctors have turned to writing both before and after his time, but not to writing like his. Whatever else Chekhov may have had, nobody able to read can doubt his extreme literary sensibility. Other writers may have been as acutely observant as he was, others may have known his wealth of social experience, others again may have shared his broad compassion, his tenderness with all genuine suffering; but where else is all this combined with so exquisite a sense, amounting to genius, of what must be said and what can be left out, of a setting, an atmosphere, a situation, a character, all presented in the fewest possible strokes? We have then at one end of this man's personality the approach and methods of science and at the other end the most delicate antennae in Russian literature. He is lancing (for nothing) peasants' boils in the morning, planning a garden, a school, a library, in the afternoon, and writing a little masterpiece at night. And all done without dogmatism and theorizing and bitterly-held ideology; all done with delicacy and gentle humour and compassion. So I say again that here was the model for a new kind of man, but the mould was broken before our blind mad century was five years old. There has only been one Anton Chekhov.

Summary of Events

1860: Jan. 17. Anton Chekhov born at Taganrog

1875: Elder brothers Alexander and Nicolai leave for Moscow

1876: Father faces bankruptcy and flees to Moscow. Mother soon follows with three younger children

Anton remains behind to continue schooling

1879: Summer. Success in school final exams and enters Moscow University

1881: Assassination of Czar Alexander II

Death of Dostoevsky

1883: First symptoms of tuberculosis

Death of Turgenev

1884: Graduates as Doctor of Medicine

1885: Practising in Moscow

The Shooting Party

1885–6 are two of most prolific years for short stories

1886: Invited to St Petersburg

Meets Suvorin, later to be his friend and publisher

Summer. Publishes *Motley Tales*

1887: Revisits Taganrog and travels to the Don Steppe.

Begins *The Steppe: The Story of a Journey*

Visits Ukraine and the Crimea

Nov. *Ivanov* is produced in Moscow

1889: Jan. *Ivanov* opens in St Petersburg

A Dreary Story

Nicolai Chekhov dies

Begins work on the *Wood Demon (Uncle Vanya)*

Wood Demon fails in Moscow

1890: April. Travels across Siberia to Sakhalin

Oct. Returns via Hong Kong, Singapore, Ceylon, Constantinople and Odessa

1891: mid-March. Sets out with Suvorin for Vienna, Venice, Nice, Monte Carlo and Paris

The Chekhov family summer in Bogimovo

The Duel

The Grasshopper

1891-2: Winter. Russia threatened with famine

1892: Helps with famine relief

Resolves to buy country estate and purchases Melikhovo

1894: early. Visits Yalta

A Woman's Kingdom Tales and Stories published

1895: Finishes first version of *The Seagull*

First visit to Tolstoy

1896: Visits Caucasus and Crimea

The Seagull produced in St Petersburg

Disaster Text published soon afterwards

1897: Feb. In Moscow involved in scheme to build 'People's Palace'

Meets Stanislavsky

Summer. Formation of the Moscow Art Theatre

Winter. Biarritz and Nice

1898: March–May. In Paris

Buys land in Yalta to build house

Visited by Bunin and Gorky at Yalta

Dec. 17. *The Seagull* opens in Moscow Art Theatre. Success

Changes publisher. Marx takes over from Suvorin

1899: Spring. *The Wood Demon* transformed into *Uncle Vanya*

Offered to Maly Theatre before being given to Moscow Art Theatre

The Lady with the Dog

Summer. Holidays with Olga Knipper in South

Oct. *Uncle Vanya* opens

Sister Masha spends Christmas vacation with him at Yalta

1900: Elected to Moscow Academy of Sciences

Moscow Art Theatre arranges Crimean tour and visits Yalta

He visits Moscow and then tours Caucasus with Gorky

July. Olga visits Chekhovs

Begins writing *The Three Sisters*

Oct. First draft finished

Finished the play in Nice

1901: Jan. 31. *The Three Sisters* opens

Returns via Italy to Yalta where he is joined by Bunin

Moscow Art Theatre goes to Petersburg

May. Anton and Olga marry secretly in Moscow

Honeymoon in Ufa before returning to Yalta

August. Olga returns to Moscow for rehearsals. Anton soon follows her and attends final rehearsals of *The Three Sisters* which opens again Sept. 21

After four weeks returns to Yalta for winter. Often sees Tolstoy

1902: end March. Olga suffers miscarriage and joins him in Yalta

April. *The Bishop*
The Betrothed

May. They return to Moscow together

June. Anton visits the Urals. They summer outside Moscow

Olga returns to Moscow to act, Anton to Yalta to write

1903: Spring. Begins *The Cherry Orchard* by Autumn. Completed and revised

Oct. Gives it to the theatre

Dec. In Moscow to attend rehearsals

1904: Jan. 17. First Night. Chekhov's forty-fourth birthday

Play not very well received, but soon after a success in St Petersburg

Feb. Returns to Yalta

May. Rejoins Olga in Moscow

They leave for Berlin to visit specialist

June. Settle in Badenweiler, a spa in Black Forest.

end June. Has a heart attack

July 2. Dies

A Select Bibliography

de Mauny, Erik (translator). *A Life of Chekhov*. Grey Walls Press.

Garnett, Constance (translator). *Letters to his Family and Friends*. Chatto & Windus.

——. *Select Tales of Tchehov*. Chatto & Windus.

——. *The Cherry Orchard and Other Plays*, Vol. I. Chatto & Windus.

——. *The Three Sisters and Other Plays*, Vol. II. Chatto & Windus.

Gorky, Maxim. *Reminiscence of Tolstoy, Chekhov and Andreev*. Hogarth Press.

Hingley, Ronald. *Chekhov: A Biographical and Critical Study*. Allen & Unwin.

Koteliansky, S. S. and Woolf, Leonard (translators). *The Notebooks of Anton Chekhov*. Hogarth Press.

Magarshack, David. *Chekhov: A Life*. Faber.

——. *Chekhov the Dramatist*. MacGibbon & Kee.

Simmons, Ernest J. *Chekhov: A Biography*. Cape.